Rich in the Making

Your Action Plan for Financial Freedom

in the AI-Powered Digital Age

Jonathan R Whitestone

Eclipse Wolf Publishing

Rich in the Making

Title: *Rich in the Making: Your Action Plan for Financial Freedom in the AI-Powered Digital Age*
Author: Jonathan R. Whitestone
Publisher: Eclipse Wolf Publishing
Publication Date: 2024
Edition: First Edition
Location: New York

Copyright © 2024

All rights reserved. No part of this book may be reproduced, stored, or transmitted in any form or by any means without prior written permission from the author or publisher.

Printed in the United States of America.

Disclaimer

The information provided in this book is for informational purposes only and should not be considered as investment or financial advice. Before making any investment decisions or expenditures, you should seek professional advice from your bank, certified financial advisors, or investment consultancy firms. The content of this book is of a general nature and is not tailored to individual financial circumstances or objectives. Therefore, it should not be relied upon as specific advice for personal investments or expenditures.

Contents

Introduction
The Digital Money Revolution
7

Chapter One
Rewiring Your Money Mindset
24

Chapter Two
Mastering the Art of Mindful Spending
57

Chapter Three
Navigating the Debt Maze
103

Chapter Four
Building Your Financial Fortress
154

Chapter Five
Investing in the Digital Age
183

Chapter Six
Mastering the Gig Economy
222

Chapter Seven
The Art of Career Hacking
255

Chapter Eight
Relationships and Money
276

Chapter Nine
Financial Wellness and Mental Health
308

Chapter Ten
Future-Proofing Your Finances
334

"Disclaimer

The information provided in this book is for informational purposes only and should not be considered as investment or financial advice. Before making any investment decisions or expenditures, you should seek professional advice from your bank, certified financial advisors, or investment consultancy firms. The content of this book is of a general nature and is not tailored to individual financial circumstances or objectives. Therefore, it should not be relied upon as specific advice for personal investments or expenditures."

Jonathan R Whitestone

Introduction: The Digital Money Revolution

Welcome to the financial frontier of the 21st century!

Imagine waking up one day to find that your entire paycheck has been deposited into a digital wallet, your investment portfolio is being managed by an AI, and your favorite coffee shop now accepts cryptocurrency. Sound far-fetched? Well, buckle up, because this is the reality we're rapidly approaching. If you're holding this book, you're probably feeling a mix of excitement and trepidation about your financial future.

Trust me, I get it. As a millennial who's ridden the rollercoaster of modern finance, I'm here to be your guide through this wild and wonderful world of digital money.

Remember when managing your finances meant balancing a checkbook and stuffing cash into envelopes? Those days are as outdated as dial-up internet. We're living in an era where you can invest in fractional shares of your favorite companies while waiting for your avocado toast, apply for a mortgage from your smartphone, and even buy digital art with cryptocurrency. It's a brave new world out there, and it's time we equipped ourselves to thrive in it.

But here's the thing: while technology has transformed the financial landscape faster than you can say "blockchain," the fundamental principles of building wealth and achieving financial well-being haven't changed. What has changed is how we apply these principles in a digital age. That's where this book comes in.

"Rich in the Making" isn't just another run-of-the-mill money guide. It's Your Action Plan for Financial Freedom in the AI-Powered Digital Age and well-being that combines time-tested financial wisdom with cutting-edge technology and a dash of behavioral economics. We're going to rewire your money mindset, master the art of mindful spending, and navigate the debt maze. We'll build your financial fortress, dive into digital investing, and even explore how your finances impact your mental health.

Now, I know what you're thinking. "Great, another finance guru promising to make me rich overnight." Let me stop you right there. *This book isn't about get-rich-quick schemes or penny-pinching your way to misery. It's about empowering you to make informed financial decisions that align with your values and goals.* It's about using technology as a tool, not a crutch. And most importantly, it's about achieving true financial independence in a world where the rules of the game seem to change daily.

Let's talk about some common misconceptions. Many people believe that you need a hefty inheritance or a six-figure salary to achieve financial success. Not true. Others think that investing is only for the wealthy or that you need to be a math whiz to manage your money effectively. Also not true. And don't even get me started on the myth that all debt is bad. We'll debunk these and many other financial fallacies throughout this book.

Here's a sobering statistic: according to a 2022 Bankrate survey, only 44% of Americans have enough savings to cover a $1,000 emergency expense. That's a problem, but it's also an opportunity. With the right knowledge and tools, we can change that narrative.

So, why is this book different? Why should you trust me to guide you through the complex world of modern finance? Well, for starters, I've been in your shoes. I've navigated the gig economy, wrestled with student loan debt, and tried to make sense of cryptocurrencies and NFTs. I've made mistakes, learned valuable lessons, and come out the other side with a deep understanding of what it takes to achieve financial success in today's world.

But it's not just about my personal experience. This book is the result of years of research, interviews with financial experts, and insights from behavioral economics. We'll be drawing on the latest studies and data to give you a comprehensive understanding of personal finance in the digital age.

One of the unique aspects of this book is its holistic approach. We're not just going to talk about numbers and spreadsheets (although we'll definitely cover those too). We're going to explore the psychology of money, the impact of financial stress on mental health, and how to align your spending with your values. Because true financial mastery isn't just about growing your bank account – it's about creating a life of purpose and fulfillment.

Let me share a quick story to illustrate what I mean. A few years ago, I met Sarah, a talented graphic designer who was struggling to make ends meet. She was working long hours at a job she hated, constantly stressed about money, and felt like she was on a financial treadmill – running fast but going nowhere. Sound familiar?

Sarah's turning point came when she realized that her approach to money was fundamentally flawed. She was so focused on cutting costs and pinching pennies that she had lost sight of the bigger picture – her overall quality of life and long-term goals. With some guidance, Sarah started to shift her mindset. Instead of just trying to spend less, she focused on earning more by leveraging her skills in the gig economy. She learned to invest in low-cost index funds, taking advantage of the power of compound interest. And most importantly, she aligned her spending with her values, cutting out expenses that didn't bring her joy and redirecting that money towards experiences and goals that truly mattered to her.

Fast forward two years, and Sarah's financial life has been transformed. She's built a thriving freelance business, has a growing investment portfolio, and is well on her way to financial independence. But here's the kicker – she's not just richer in terms of money. She's happier, less stressed, and feels in control of her financial future.

Sarah's story illustrates **three key principles** that we'll explore in depth throughout this book:

1. Mindset is everything: Your beliefs about money shape your financial reality. By changing your mindset, you can change your financial life.

2. Technology is a tool, not a solution: The digital age offers incredible tools for managing and growing your money, but they're only effective if you use them wisely.

3. Holistic wealth is the goal: True financial mastery isn't just about accumulating money – it's about creating a life of purpose, fulfillment, and financial freedom.

Throughout this book, you'll find practical exercises, real-life case studies, and actionable advice that you can implement right away. We'll also be looking at how technology is reshaping the financial landscape and how you can use these tools to your advantage.

For example, did you know that there are now apps that can analyze your spending patterns and suggest areas where you might be able to save money? Or that you can use AI-powered tools to optimize your investment portfolio? We'll explore these and many other cutting-edge financial technologies throughout the book.

But it's not all about high-tech solutions. We'll also be diving into timeless financial principles and showing you how to apply them in today's world. We'll talk about the importance of living below your means, the power of compound interest, and why diversification is still one of the most important principles in investing.

One of the things I'm most excited about in this book is our exploration of the gig economy and how to thrive financially in a world of flexible work. Whether you're a full-time freelancer or just looking to start a side hustle, we'll cover strategies for managing irregular income, maximizing your earning potential, and navigating the unique tax challenges that come with self-employment.

We'll also be tackling some of the biggest financial challenges facing our generation. Student loan debt? We've got a whole chapter dedicated to strategies for paying it off faster. Worried about saving for retirement when you're just trying to make rent? We'll show you how to start small and build momentum over time.

And let's not forget about the elephant in the room – the housing market. Whether you're hoping to buy your first home or you're wondering if homeownership is even a realistic goal, we'll explore your options and help you make an informed decision.

Throughout the book, we'll be hearing from a variety of experts in different fields. We'll have insights from financial planners, tech entrepreneurs, psychologists, and even futurists who are predicting the next big trends in personal finance. These expert contributions will give you a well-rounded perspective on the complex world of money.

But perhaps the most important aspect of this book is its focus on you. Your goals, your values, your unique financial situation. Because here's the truth: there's no one-size-fits-all approach to financial success. What works for your friend or your parents might not work for you. That's why we'll be providing tools and frameworks to help you create a personalized financial plan that aligns with your life goals.

Now, let's dive a bit deeper into **what you can expect from each chapter of this book:**

1. Rewiring Your Money Mindset: In this chapter, we'll explore the psychological aspects of money. We'll look at how your upbringing, experiences, and beliefs shape your relationship with money. You'll learn how to identify and overcome limiting beliefs that might be holding you back financially. We'll also introduce you to the concept of a "money script" – the unconscious beliefs about money that guide your financial decisions. By the end of this chapter, you'll have the tools to rewrite your money script and develop a healthier, more empowering relationship with money.

2. Mastering the Art of Mindful Spending: This isn't about extreme frugality or depriving yourself. Instead, we'll explore how to align your spending with your values and long-term goals. You'll learn how to create a values-based spending plan that allows you to enjoy life now while still planning for the future. We'll also dive into the psychology of spending, exploring concepts like hedonic adaptation and the paradox of choice. You'll come away with practical strategies for making more intentional spending decisions and leveraging technology to support your goals.

3. Navigating the Debt Maze: Debt can be a powerful tool when used wisely, but it can also be a major obstacle to financial freedom. In this chapter, we'll explore different types of debt and strategies for managing them effectively. You'll learn how to prioritize debt repayment, negotiate with creditors, and use technology to accelerate your debt payoff. We'll also discuss the emotional aspects of debt and how to stay motivated on your debt-free journey.

4. Building Your Financial Fortress: An emergency fund is the foundation of financial security, but it's just the beginning. In this chapter, we'll explore how to create a comprehensive financial safety net. We'll cover everything from insurance (including often-overlooked types like disability insurance) to estate planning. You'll learn how to determine the right size emergency fund for your situation and where to keep it for easy access and growth.

5. Investing in the Digital Age: Investing can seem intimidating, especially with all the new options available. We'll break down the basics of investing and explore how technology has democratized access to the markets. You'll learn about different types of investments, from stocks and bonds to real estate investment trusts (REITs) and cryptocurrency. We'll also dive into the world of robo-advisors and discuss when they might (or might not) be the right choice for you.

6. Mastering the Gig Economy: The world of work is changing, and this chapter will help you navigate the financial challenges and opportunities of the gig economy. We'll cover strategies for managing irregular income, maximizing your earning potential, and handling taxes as a freelancer or independent contractor. You'll also learn about the importance of personal branding and how to leverage platforms like LinkedIn to find opportunities.

7. The Art of Career Hacking: Your career is your most valuable financial asset, and this chapter will help you maximize its potential. We'll explore strategies for negotiating your salary, identifying high-value skills to develop, and navigating career transitions. You'll learn how to create a personal development plan that aligns with your financial goals and how to leverage online learning platforms to upskill affordably.

8. Sustainable and Ethical Investing: More and more people are looking to align their investments with their values. In this chapter, we'll explore the world of ESG (Environmental, Social, and Governance) investing. You'll learn how to evaluate companies and funds based on their sustainability practices and social impact. We'll also discuss the potential returns and risks of sustainable investing and how to incorporate these principles into your overall investment strategy.

9. Relationships and Money: Money is one of the leading causes of stress in relationships. This chapter will provide strategies for navigating financial decisions with partners, family members, and even friends. We'll discuss how to have productive money conversations, how to merge finances (or keep them separate) in a relationship, and how to teach kids about money in the digital age.

10. Financial Wellness and Mental Health: Your financial health and mental health are closely linked. In this chapter, we'll explore the connection between money and well-being. You'll learn strategies for managing financial stress, cultivating a positive money mindset, and finding balance between financial goals and overall life satisfaction. We'll also discuss when and how to seek professional help for financial stress or anxiety.

11. Future-Proofing Your Finances: The financial world is constantly evolving, and this chapter will help you prepare for what's next. We'll explore emerging trends like decentralized finance (DeFi), central bank digital currencies, and the potential impact of artificial intelligence on personal finance. You'll learn strategies for staying adaptable and resilient in the face of economic uncertainty.

Throughout the book, you'll find plenty of real-life examples and case studies to illustrate key concepts. For instance, you'll meet Mark and Lisa, a couple who managed to pay off $50,000 in debt in just two years by applying the strategies we'll discuss. Their story will show you that no matter how deep in debt you might be, there's always a path forward.

We'll also be busting some common financial myths along the way. For example, did you know that carrying a balance on your credit card doesn't actually improve your credit score? Or that buying a house isn't always better than renting? We'll separate fact from fiction and give you the knowledge you need to make informed decisions.

One of the unique features of this book is our "Tech Spotlight" sections, where we'll dive deep into a specific financial technology and show you how to use it effectively. From budgeting apps to robo-advisors, we'll cover the tools that can make your financial life easier and more efficient.

We'll also have *"Action Steps"* at the end of each chapter – concrete tasks you can complete to start implementing what you've learned right away. These might include things like setting up automatic savings transfers, researching investment options, or having a money conversation with your partner.

Remember, financial mastery isn't about perfection. It's about progress. It's about making informed decisions, learning from your mistakes, and continuously adapting to a changing world. So don't worry if you feel overwhelmed at times – that's normal. The key is to take it one step at a time and celebrate your progress along the way.

As we wrap up this introduction, I want to leave you with a thought. Money is a tool, not an end in itself. The goal of this book isn't just to help you accumulate wealth, but to use that wealth to create a life that's meaningful and fulfilling to you. Whether that means traveling the world, starting a business, supporting causes you care about, or simply having the peace of mind that comes with financial security – that's up to you.

So, are you ready to take control of your financial future? Are you ready to master your money in the digital age? Let's get started on this exciting journey together. Turn the page, and let's begin your path to financial mastery!

Before we dive into the first chapter, let's take a moment to set the stage for your financial journey. Here's a *quick exercise* to get you started:

1. Grab a pen and paper (or open a note-taking app on your phone).
2. Write down your top three financial goals. They can be short-term (like saving for a vacation) or long-term (like retiring comfortably).
3. Next to each goal, jot down one thing that's currently holding you back from achieving it.
4. Finally, write down one small step you could take this week to move closer to each goal.

This simple exercise will help you start thinking about your financial future in concrete terms. We'll be revisiting and refining these goals throughout the book, so don't worry if they're not perfect. The important thing is to start the process of actively engaging with your finances.

As we move through the chapters, you'll notice that each one builds on the last, creating a comprehensive framework for financial mastery. But don't feel like you need to read the book in order. If there's a particular topic that's pressing for you right now, feel free to jump to that chapter first. The book is designed to be both a step-by-step guide and a reference that you can return to as your financial needs and goals evolve.

You'll also find that throughout the book, we emphasize the importance of taking action. Knowledge is power, but it's only through consistent action that we can create real change in our financial lives. That's why each chapter includes practical exercises and action steps. I encourage you to actually do these exercises – don't just read about them. The more you engage with the material, the more you'll get out of this book.

Finally, I want to acknowledge that everyone's financial journey is unique. Your starting point, your goals, and your challenges are your own. This book isn't about comparing yourself to others or trying to achieve some arbitrary definition of financial success. It's about empowering you to create a financial life that aligns with your values and supports your vision for the future.

What You'll Learn in Chapter 1: Rewiring Your Money Mindset

In the next chapter, we'll dive deep into the psychology of money. You'll learn:

- How to identify your current money beliefs and where they come from
- The impact of your money mindset on your financial decisions
- Techniques for overcoming limiting beliefs about money
- How to develop a growth mindset

Chapter 1: Rewiring Your Money Mindset

Picture this: You're scrolling through Instagram, and suddenly you're hit with an ad for the latest must-have gadget. Your finger hovers over the "Buy Now" button, and before you know it, you've added it to your cart. But when it comes to investing in your future or saving for that dream vacation, you freeze faster than a computer running Windows 95. Why is it so easy to spend on immediate gratification but so hard to invest in our long-term well-being?

Welcome to the digital money revolution, where your smartphone is your bank, your watch is your wallet, and your favorite influencer might just be your financial advisor. (Spoiler alert: Please don't take financial advice from TikTok. Just... don't.)

In this brave new world of finance, your money mindset is like the operating system of your financial life. It's running in the background, influencing every financial choice you make, often without you even realizing it. And just like that ancient laptop you've been meaning to upgrade, sometimes our money mindsets need a serious reboot.

So, grab your virtual reality headsets, because we're about to take a deep dive into the psychology of money in the digital age. We'll explore where your money beliefs come from, how they impact your financial decisions, and most importantly, how to rewire them for greater financial success and well-being. Think of it as a software update for your brain – Money Mindset 2.0, if you will.

Understanding Your Money Story

Let's start with a simple truth: Your relationship with money didn't begin when you opened your first bank account or received your first paycheck. It started much earlier, shaped by the experiences, observations, and messages you absorbed growing up. It's like the origin story of a superhero, except instead of getting bitten by a radioactive spider, you got bitten by the money bug.

Think back to your childhood. What did you learn about money from your parents or guardians? Were financial discussions open and positive, or were they fraught with tension and secrecy? Did you grow up with abundance, or was there a constant worry about making ends meet? Was money talked about as often as the weather, or was it treated like Voldemort – the topic that must not be named?

These early experiences form what financial psychologists call your "money script" – the unconscious beliefs about money that guide your financial decisions. It's like the source code of your financial operating system. Here are some common *money scripts*:

1. Money Avoidance: "Money is the root of all evil." People with this script often struggle to save or plan for the future.

They're like the Frodos of finance, trying to throw their money into Mount Doom.

2. Money Worship: "More money will solve all my problems." This can lead to overspending and debt accumulation. These folks are the Tony Starks of finance – they think throwing money at a problem will fix everything.

3. Money Status: "My self-worth is tied to my net worth." This often results in competitive spending and financial stress. They're the Instagram influencers of finance, always chasing the next big thing to show off.

4. Money Vigilance: "I must always be prepared for financial emergencies." While this can lead to good saving habits, it might also cause excessive anxiety about spending. These are the Batman types – always prepared, but maybe a little too paranoid.

Let's dive deeper into each of these money scripts and explore how they might manifest in real-life situations:

Money Avoidance:
People with this script often have a complicated relationship with money. They might feel guilty about having money or

believe that wanting more money is somehow wrong or greedy. This can lead to self-sabotaging behaviors like:

- Neglecting to check bank balances or pay bills on time (because ignorance is bliss, right?)
- Avoiding financial planning or discussions about money (like it's a game of financial hide-and-seek)
- Underearning or staying in low-paying jobs despite having valuable skills (because who needs a raise when you can have moral superiority?)
- Giving money away, even when they can't afford to (because nothing says "I'm not greedy" like an empty bank account)

For example, Sarah, a talented graphic designer, consistently undercharges for her work because she feels uncomfortable asking for more money. As a result, she struggles to make ends meet, reinforcing her belief that money is a source of stress and anxiety. It's like she's playing a game of financial limbo – how low can you go?

Money Worship:
This script is often rooted in the belief that money is the answer to all of life's problems. While having sufficient financial resources can certainly alleviate many stresses, this belief can lead to:

- Prioritizing making money over other important aspects of life, like relationships or health (because who needs friends when you have a fat bank account?)
- Overspending in the belief that the next purchase will bring happiness (spoiler alert: it won't)
- Taking on excessive debt to maintain a certain lifestyle (because nothing says "living the dream" like crushing debt)
- Difficulty finding satisfaction, always chasing the next financial milestone (it's like playing Pac-Man with dollar signs)

Consider Tom, who grew up in a low-income household. He now has a high-paying job but finds himself constantly working overtime and missing important family events. He believes that if he can just make enough money, everything in his life will be perfect. Spoiler alert: It won't be, Tom. Put down the spreadsheet and pick up the phone – call your mom.

Money Status:
This script equates net worth with self-worth. People with this belief often:

- Engage in competitive or conspicuous spending to "keep up with the Joneses" (or the Kardashians, depending on your aspirations)

- Make financial decisions based on how they'll be perceived by others (because nothing says "I've made it" like a luxury car you can't afford)
- Struggle with feelings of shame or inadequacy if they can't afford certain things (cue the world's smallest violin)
- Have difficulty saying no to social events or purchases that strain their budget (FOMO is expensive, folks)

Lisa, for instance, maxed out her credit cards buying designer clothes and dining at expensive restaurants because she believed it was necessary to fit in with her coworkers. She's now dealing with significant debt and stress. Remember, Lisa: The most stylish accessory is a positive bank balance.

Money Vigilance:
While being cautious with money can be positive, extreme vigilance can lead to:

- Excessive worry about financial security, even when objectively stable (it's like having a financial security blanket... made of anxiety)
- Difficulty enjoying money or spending on pleasurable experiences (because fun is overrated, right?)

- Hoarding money at the expense of meeting current needs (Scrooge McDuck, is that you?)
- Lack of transparency about finances with family members (because nothing says "I love you" like financial secrecy)

Mike, for example, grew up during an economic recession and now saves every penny he can. Despite having a healthy emergency fund and retirement savings, he still loses sleep worrying about potential financial disasters and rarely allows himself or his family any "unnecessary" expenses. Mike, my friend, it's time to loosen up that financial straitjacket a bit.

Exercise: Identifying Your Money Script

Take a moment to reflect on your own money beliefs. Which of the above scripts resonate with you? Or do you have a different set of beliefs altogether? Write down three to five money beliefs you hold, no matter how irrational they might seem. For example:
- "I'll never be good with money." (Ah, the classic self-fulfilling prophecy)
- "Rich people are greedy." (Because generalizations are always accurate, right?)
- "I don't deserve financial success." (Says who? The committee of voices in your head?)

Now, for each belief, try to trace its origin. Did it come from something your parents said? A childhood experience? Societal messages? Understanding where these beliefs come from is the first step in challenging and changing them. It's like being a detective in the mystery of your own financial psyche.

The Impact of Your Money Mindset

Your money mindset isn't just abstract psychology – it has real, tangible effects on your financial life. It's like the butterfly effect, but instead of a butterfly flapping its wings and causing a hurricane, it's your beliefs about money causing a storm in your bank account.

Let's look at how different mindsets can play out in real-world scenarios:

Scarcity Mindset vs. Abundance Mindset

Sarah and Mike are both 28-year-old marketing professionals earning similar salaries. Sarah grew up in a household where money was tight, and financial discussions were always tense. As a result, she developed a scarcity mindset – a belief that there's never enough money to go around. It's like she's always playing a game of financial musical chairs, afraid the music will stop and she'll be left without a seat.

Mike, on the other hand, grew up in a middle-class family where money was discussed openly and positively. He developed an abundance mindset – a belief that there are always opportunities to earn and grow wealth. He sees the financial world as a buffet of opportunities, not a fight for the last slice of pizza.

How does this play out in their lives?

Sarah:
- Hesitates to negotiate her salary, fearing she might lose her job (because asking for what you're worth is totally a fireable offense, right?)
- Avoids investing, seeing it as too risky (because stuffing cash under your mattress is a solid retirement plan)
- Feels guilty about any non-essential purchases (sorry, avocado toast, you're on the chopping block)
- Often feels stressed and anxious about money (her theme song? "Mo Money Mo Problems")

Mike:

- Regularly negotiates for raises and better benefits (because closed mouths don't get fed... or paid)
- Invests a portion of his income, seeing it as an opportunity for growth (his money doesn't just sit there, it does push-ups)
- Budgets for both necessities and enjoyment (because all work and no play makes Mike a dull boy)
- Feels generally positive and in control of his finances (his theme song? "I've Got the Power")

The result? Five years down the line, Mike has a higher salary, a growing investment portfolio, and feels confident about his financial future. Sarah, despite having similar skills and starting at the same point, is still living paycheck to paycheck and feeling stuck. It's like they started on the same financial game board, but Mike's playing Monopoly while Sarah's stuck in Snakes and Ladders.

This example illustrates how your money mindset can create a self-fulfilling prophecy. A scarcity mindset can lead to missed opportunities and financial stagnation, while an abundance mindset can open doors and create positive financial momentum. It's like the financial version of "The Secret" – minus the questionable pseudoscience.

Let's delve deeper into the characteristics of scarcity and abundance *mindsets*:

Scarcity Mindset:
- Focuses on what's lacking or missing (glass half empty, anyone?)
- Views resources as limited and finite (as if we're all fighting over the last cookie in the jar)
- Leads to fear-based decision making (because nothing says "smart choices" like panic, right?)
- Often results in a "zero-sum" game mentality (if you win, I must lose)
- Can cause stress, anxiety, and feelings of helplessness (fun times!)

Abundance Mindset:
- Focuses on opportunities and possibilities (glass half full, and hey, we can always get more water!)
- Views resources as plentiful and renewable (there's enough pie for everyone, and we can bake more!)
- Leads to opportunity-based decision making (because fortune favors the bold... and the financially savvy)
- Embraces a "rising tide lifts all boats" mentality (your success doesn't diminish mine)
- Promotes creativity, optimism, and resilience (because life's too short for financial doom and gloom)

It's important to note that having an abundance mindset doesn't mean ignoring financial realities or being reckless with money. Instead, it's about approaching your finances with a sense of possibility and empowerment, rather than fear and limitation. It's the difference between saying "I can't afford that" and "How can I afford that?"

Fixed Mindset vs. Growth Mindset

Another crucial aspect of your money mindset is whether you have a fixed or growth mindset when it comes to financial skills. This concept, pioneered by psychologist Carol Dweck, applies to finances just as much as it does to other areas of life.

Someone with a fixed mindset might think:
- "I'm just not good with numbers, so I'll never be good with money." (Because apparently, financial skills are encoded in our DNA)
- "Financial success is for other people, not for me." (Did you miss the memo that said you're excluded from wealth?)
- "I've always been bad with money, and that's just how it is." (Because people never change, right? Just ask my high school yearbook photo)

On the other hand, someone with a growth mindset might think:
- "I may not understand investing now, but I can learn." (Hello, YouTube tutorials and finance podcasts!)
- "Every financial mistake is an opportunity to gain knowledge and do better next time." (It's not a failure, it's a learning experience with a price tag)
- "My financial skills can improve with effort and education." (Your brain is like a muscle – the more you use it, the stronger it gets)

A growth mindset is crucial for financial success because it empowers you to learn, adapt, and improve your financial situation over time. It's like having a financial superpower – the ability to level up your money skills!

Let's explore how these mindsets might play out in a real-life scenario:

Emma and Jack are both 25 and starting their first jobs out of college. They each receive a signing bonus and want to start investing.

Emma has a fixed mindset about finances. She thinks, "I've never been good with money, and investing seems complicated. I'll probably just lose it all." As a result, she leaves her bonus sitting in a low-interest savings account, missing out on potential growth. It's like she's leaving her money in the kiddie pool when it could be doing laps in the Olympic-sized pool of the stock market.

Jack, with his growth mindset, thinks, "I don't know much about investing yet, but I can learn." He spends time researching, asks questions, and eventually invests his bonus in a diversified portfolio of low-cost index funds. Over time, even if he makes some mistakes, Jack's willingness to learn and adapt will likely lead to better financial outcomes. He's playing the long game, while Emma's stuck on the sidelines.

The Power of Financial Self-Efficacy

Closely related to the concept of mindset is financial self-efficacy – your belief in your ability to successfully manage your money and achieve your financial goals. It's like your financial confidence muscle – the stronger it is, the more financial heavy lifting you can do.

People with high financial self-efficacy are more likely to:
- Take control of their finances rather than avoiding them (no more hiding bills under the mattress!)

- Seek out financial education and advice (because knowledge is power, and power is money... or something like that)
- Persist in the face of financial challenges (when the going gets tough, the financially self-efficacious get going)
- Make proactive financial decisions (they're the captains of their financial ships, not just passengers)

On the other hand, low financial self-efficacy can lead to:
- Procrastination on important financial tasks (because nothing says "adulting" like ignoring your finances, right?)
- Feeling overwhelmed or helpless about money matters (cue the dramatic fainting couch)
- Avoiding financial decisions or defaulting to others' advice without question (because blindly following the herd always works out well)
- Giving up easily when faced with financial setbacks (throwing in the towel faster than a boxer in a rigged fight)

Building financial self-efficacy is a crucial part of developing a healthy money mindset. It involves not just acquiring knowledge, but also gaining confidence through experience and celebrating small financial wins along the way. It's like leveling up in a video game – each small victory builds your skills and confidence for the bigger challenges ahead.

Exercise: Challenging Your Money Mindset

Now that we've explored different aspects of money mindsets, it's time to put on your detective hat and investigate your own beliefs. Look back at the money beliefs you wrote down earlier. For each one, ask yourself:

1. Is this belief based on fact or assumption? (Spoiler alert: It's probably an assumption)
2. How is this belief helping or hindering my financial progress? (Is it a financial booster rocket or an anchor?)
3. What would be a more empowering belief to hold instead? (Time for a belief makeover!)

For example, if you believe "I'll never be good with money," you might challenge it like this:

1. Is this based on fact or assumption? Assumption. I've never really tried to learn about money management.
2. How is this hindering me? It's stopping me from even trying to improve my finances. (Talk about self-sabotage, right?)
3. A more empowering belief: "I can learn to manage money effectively with time and effort." (Look at you, growth mindset champion!)

Rewiring Your Money Mindset

Now that we've identified and challenged some of our existing money beliefs, let's talk about how to rewire our money mindset for greater financial success and well-being. Think of it as a software update for your brain – Money Mindset 2.0, if you will.

1. Cultivate Financial Self-Awareness

The first step in rewiring your money mindset is to become more aware of your financial thoughts and behaviors. Start paying attention to the emotions that come up when you think about money. Do you feel anxiety? Excitement? Shame? Are you more Scrooge McDuck or Rebecca Bloomwood from Confessions of a Shopaholic?

Also, notice your automatic financial behaviors. Do you check your bank balance regularly, or do you avoid it like that one relative at family gatherings? Do you plan your purchases, or do you tend to buy impulsively?

Exercise: Financial Mindfulness

For the next week, keep a "money journal." Each day, write down:

- Any financial decisions you made (even small ones like buying coffee)
- The emotions you felt while making these decisions
- Any money-related thoughts that popped into your head

This exercise can help you identify patterns in your financial thinking and behavior, making it easier to spot areas for improvement. It's like being a detective in the mystery of your own financial psyche.

2. Educate Yourself

A key component of a healthy money mindset is financial literacy. The more you understand about personal finance, the more confident and empowered you'll feel. And in this digital age, there's no shortage of resources at your fingertips.

Start small – pick one financial topic you want to learn more about, whether it's budgeting, investing, or credit scores. Find a reputable book, podcast, or online course on the subject and commit to spending 15 minutes a day learning about it.

Here are some tech-savvy ways to boost your financial education:

- Use apps like Investopedia's financial term glossary to learn new concepts on the go.
- Follow financial experts on social media platforms like Twitter or LinkedIn for daily insights.
- Take advantage of free online courses from platforms like Coursera or edX on personal finance topics.
- Use YouTube channels like "Two Cents" or "The Financial Diet" for engaging, easy-to-understand financial content.

Remember, financial education is a lifelong journey. The financial world is always evolving, and there's always more to learn. Embrace this as an exciting opportunity for growth, not an overwhelming task. You're not trying to become the next Warren Buffett overnight (unless you are, in which case, can I be your friend?).

3. Practice Positive Money Affirmations

Affirmations are positive statements that can help reshape your thinking patterns over time. Think of them as the yoga of the mind – stretching your beliefs into more positive positions. Here are some money affirmations you might find helpful:

- "I am capable of making smart financial decisions."
- "Money flows into my life easily and abundantly."
- "I deserve financial success and stability."
- "I am learning and improving my money management skills every day."
- "My bank account is as healthy as Thor's biceps."

Choose one or two affirmations that resonate with you and repeat them to yourself daily, perhaps as part of your morning routine or before making financial decisions. You might feel a bit silly at first, but hey, if it works for Olympic athletes and CEOs, it can work for your finances too!

4. Surround Yourself with Positive Financial Influences

The people we spend time with can have a significant impact on our mindset and behaviors. Try to connect with people who have healthy money habits and positive attitudes towards finance. It's like creating your own personal Avengers team, but for money management.

This doesn't mean you need to ditch your friends who are struggling financially. Instead, consider joining a personal finance group, attending money management workshops, or finding a "money buddy" – someone you can discuss financial goals and challenges with regularly.

In the digital age, your financial influences can extend beyond your immediate circle:

- Join online communities like Reddit's r/personalfinance or Facebook groups focused on financial wellness.
- Follow financial influencers on Instagram or TikTok who share practical money tips (but remember to fact-check and not blindly follow advice).
- Use apps like Meetup to find local financial wellness groups or workshops.

5. Celebrate Financial Wins, No Matter How Small

Often, we're quick to beat ourselves up over financial missteps but slow to acknowledge our successes. Make a conscious effort to celebrate your financial wins, no matter how small they might seem.

Did you resist an impulse purchase? Celebrate it. Did you finally set up that automatic transfer to your savings account? That's worth acknowledging. By celebrating these small wins, you reinforce positive financial behaviors and build confidence in your ability to manage money.

Consider using a habit-tracking app like Habitica or Streaks to gamify your financial goals and celebrate your progress. Who says managing money can't be fun?

6. Reframe Your Relationship with Money

Instead of seeing money as a source of stress or something to be feared, try to reframe it as a tool for creating the life you want. Money isn't inherently good or bad – it's simply a resource that can be used to support your values and goals.

Exercise: Money as a Tool

Write down three ways that money can help you live a life aligned with your values. For example:
1. Money can help me support causes I care about through charitable donations.
2. Money can provide security for my family.
3. Money can allow me to pursue further education and personal growth.

By focusing on how money can support your values, you can develop a more positive and purposeful relationship with it. It's like turning money from the villain in your story to a sidekick helping you achieve your goals.

7. *Practice Gratitude*

Gratitude is a powerful tool for shifting from a scarcity mindset to an abundance mindset. Regular gratitude practice can help you focus on what you have rather than what you lack, reducing financial anxiety and promoting a more positive money mindset.

Exercise: Financial Gratitude Journal

Each day for a week, write down three things you're financially grateful for. These can be big or small. For example:
- "I'm grateful I was able to pay my bills on time this month."
- "I'm thankful for the free park near my house where I can exercise and relax."
- "I appreciate having a job that provides steady income."

You can use gratitude apps like Gratitude or ThinkUp to make this practice easier and more engaging.

8. Visualize Your Financial Success

Visualization is a powerful technique used by athletes, entrepreneurs, and other high achievers. You can apply this same technique to your financial life. It's like creating a mental vision board for your money goals.

Take some time to visualize your ideal financial future. What does it look like? How does it feel to be financially secure and successful? The more vivid and detailed you can make this visualization, the more powerful it will be in shaping your mindset and behaviors.

Exercise: Financial Vision Board

Create a vision board representing your financial goals and the life you want to create. You can do this physically with magazine cutouts or digitally using an app like Pinterest or Canva. Include images that represent your financial goals (like a dream home or a successful business) as well as the feelings you associate with financial success (peace, freedom, generosity).

Place this vision board somewhere you'll see it regularly to keep your financial goals top of mind. You can even set it as your phone or computer wallpaper for a constant reminder.

9. Embrace Financial Self-Compassion

Finally, it's crucial to practice self-compassion in your financial journey. Everyone makes money mistakes – it's part of the learning process. Instead of beating yourself up over past financial missteps, treat yourself with the same kindness you'd offer a friend.

When you make a financial mistake, try this *self-compassion exercise*:

1. *Acknowledge* the mistake without judgment: "I overspent this month."
2. *Recognize* that financial challenges are a common human experience: "Many people struggle with overspending sometimes."
3. Offer yourself *kindness*: "I'm learning to manage my money better, and it's okay to make mistakes along the way."
4. *Focus* on learning and moving forward: "What can I learn from this experience to make better choices next time?"

Remember, rewiring your money mindset is a journey, not a destination. It takes time, patience, and consistent effort to change long-held beliefs and behaviors. Be kind to yourself in the process and celebrate every step forward, no matter how small.

10. Leverage Technology for Mindset Shifts

In our digital age, there are numerous apps and tools that can support your journey to a *healthier money mindset*:

- Use *mood tracking apps* like Daylio or Moodfit to correlate your emotions with your spending habits.
- Try *meditation apps* like Headspace or Calm to reduce financial stress and anxiety.
- Use *goal-setting apps* like Strides or GoalsOnTrack to set and track your financial objectives.
- Explore *financial wellness apps* like Cleo or Digit that use AI to provide personalized financial insights and encouragement.

Remember, these tools are meant to support your journey, not replace the inner work of changing your mindset. Use them wisely, and don't forget to unplug and reflect on your progress regularly.

Putting It All Together: Your Money Mindset Action Plan

Now that we've explored various strategies for rewiring your money mindset, it's time to put it all together into an actionable plan. Here's a step-by-step guide to start transforming your relationship with money:

Week 1: Self-Reflection and Awareness
- Complete the "Identifying Your Money Script" exercise
- Start your daily "Financial Mindfulness" journal
- Take a financial self-efficacy assessment (you can find these online)

Week 2: Education and Positive Influences
- Choose a financial topic to learn about and spend 15 minutes each day studying it
- Find a "money buddy" or join a personal finance group
- Identify and follow three positive financial role models on social media

Week 3: Affirmations and Gratitude
- Choose two money affirmations to repeat daily
- Start your Financial Gratitude Journal

- Create a list of your past financial successes, no matter how small

Week 4: Visualization and Goal-Setting
- Create your Financial Vision Board
- Set one short-term and one long-term financial goal
- Write a letter to your future self, describing your ideal financial situation

Remember, changing your money mindset is an ongoing process. Revisit these exercises regularly and be patient with yourself as you work on developing a healthier relationship with money.

Self-Assessment Quiz: What's Your Money Mindset?

To help you gauge where you currently stand with your money mindset, take this quick self-assessment quiz. For each statement, rate how much you agree on a scale of 1 (strongly disagree) to 5 (strongly agree):

1. I feel confident in my ability to manage my finances.
2. I believe I can learn and improve my financial skills over time.
3. I see money as a tool to achieve my goals, not as a source of stress.
4. I'm comfortable talking about money with others.
5. I regularly set and work towards financial goals.
6. I'm aware of my spending habits and how they align with my values.
7. I view financial setbacks as learning opportunities, not failures.
8. I feel in control of my financial future.
9. I'm open to learning new financial strategies and tools.
10. I believe I deserve financial success and abundance.

Scoring:
40-50: You have a strong, positive money mindset. Keep nurturing it!

30-39: You're on the right track. Focus on areas where you scored lower.

20-29: There's room for improvement. Consider which areas you want to work on first.

10-19: Your money mindset could use some TLC. Don't worry – you've taken the first step by recognizing it!

Remember, this quiz is just a starting point. Use your results to identify areas where you might want to focus your mindset work.

Conclusion

Your money mindset is the foundation of your financial life. By understanding and rewiring your beliefs about money, you can open up new possibilities for financial success and well-being.

As we wrap up this chapter, I want to leave you with one final thought: Your current financial situation is not a reflection of your worth as a person. It's simply the result of your past decisions, which were influenced by the money mindset you held at the time. The good news is, now that you're aware of your money mindset and have tools to change it, you have the power to create a different financial future.

Remember, rewiring your money mindset is not about striving for perfection. It's about progress, self-awareness, and continuous growth. Be patient with yourself, celebrate your wins (no matter how small), and keep pushing forward. Your future self will thank you for the work you're doing now.

In the next chapter, we'll build on this foundation as we explore the art of mindful spending. We'll look at how to align your spending with your values and use technology to support conscious consumption. But for now, take some time to reflect on what you've learned about your money mindset and start implementing your action plan.

Remember, every step you take towards a healthier money mindset is a step towards greater financial mastery and overall well-being. You've got this!

Chapter 2: Mastering the Art of Mindful Spending

In a world where one-click purchases and targeted ads seem to read our minds, mastering the art of mindful spending has never been more crucial. Welcome to the digital spending frontier, where your smartphone is both your greatest ally and your potential financial nemesis.

As we dive into this chapter, remember that mindful spending isn't about depriving yourself or living like a digital-age monk. It's about aligning your spending with your values and goals, leveraging technology to make informed decisions, and creating a sustainable approach to consumption that benefits both your wallet and the planet.

The Mindful Spending Revolution in the Digital Age

Before we jump into the how-to's, let's talk about why mindful spending is more crucial now than ever. In our hyper-connected, instant-gratification world, it's easier than ever to spend money without really thinking about it. One-click ordering, contactless payments, and the ability to buy almost anything from anywhere at any time have removed many of the natural "pause points" in the spending process.

Remember when you had to physically go to a store, interact with a salesperson, and hand over cash to make a purchase? Those were all opportunities to reconsider whether you really needed or wanted something. Now, you can buy a smart toaster that tweets your breakfast preferences at 3 AM while binge-watching your favorite show, all without leaving your couch. (No judgment if you actually own a tweeting toaster. We all have our quirks.)

This ease of spending, combined with sophisticated marketing techniques and the social pressure of "keeping up with the Joneses" (or the influencers, if you're more digitally inclined), has created a perfect storm for mindless consumption. The result? Many of us are spending money in ways that don't truly align with our values or long-term goals.

But fear not! Mindful spending is here to save the day (and your bank account). By becoming more intentional about *how we use our money*, we can:

1. Reduce financial stress and anxiety: When you're in control of your spending, you're less likely to lie awake at night worrying about your finances.

2. Align our spending with our values and life goals: Your money should be a tool to create the life you want, not a source of regret.

3. Increase overall life satisfaction and well-being: Studies have shown that experiences tend to bring more lasting happiness than material possessions.

4. Save more for the things that truly matter to us: Whether it's a dream vacation, a comfortable retirement, or supporting a cause you care about, mindful spending helps you prioritize what's important.

5. *Reduce waste and environmental impact:* Conscious consumption often leads to more sustainable choices, benefiting both your wallet and the planet.

Sounds pretty good, right? Let's dive into how we can make this mindful spending magic happen in the digital age.

Creating a Tech-Savvy, Values-Based Spending Plan

The first step in mastering mindful spending is to create a spending plan that aligns with your values and goals. This isn't your grandma's budget – we're talking about a flexible, personalized approach that reflects what truly matters to you and leverages the power of technology.

Step 1: Identify Your Core Values and Life Goals

Before we start crunching numbers or downloading apps, let's take a step back and think about what really matters to you. What are your core values? What are your big life goals? These will be the foundation of your mindful spending plan.

Exercise: Values and Goals Reflection

Take a few minutes to jot down answers to these questions:

1. What are the three most important things in your life right now?
2. What do you want your life to look like in 5 years? 10 years?
3. What activities or experiences bring you the most joy and fulfillment?
4. If money were no object, how would you spend your time?
5. What causes or issues are you passionate about?

Your answers might include things like family, health, career growth, travel, environmental sustainability, or creative pursuits. There are no right or wrong answers – what matters is that they're authentic to you.

For example, you might realize that while you've been spending a lot on the latest gadgets, what really brings you joy is spending time in nature with your family. This realization could lead you to prioritize spending on outdoor gear and family trips over the newest smartphone.

Pro Tip: Use a digital journaling app like Day One or Journey to record your reflections. These apps allow you to add photos, location tags, and even voice memos, creating a rich, multimedia record of your financial journey. You can look back on these entries later to see how your values and goals have evolved over time.

Step 2: Categorize Your Expenses

Now that you have a clearer picture of what matters most to you, let's look at how your current spending aligns with these values and goals. We'll categorize your expenses into three buckets:

1. Essential: These are the non-negotiables – things you need to survive and function in society. Think rent/mortgage, utilities, basic food, healthcare, etc. These expenses form the foundation of your financial life and should be prioritized.

2. Important: These expenses align with your values and goals. They're not absolutely necessary for survival, but they contribute significantly to your well-being and long-term objectives. This might include things like education expenses, gym membership (if health is a top value), or donations to causes you care about. These expenses are where you can really start to align your spending with your values.

3. *Optional:* These are the nice-to-haves. They might bring you some joy or convenience, but they don't strongly align with your core values or contribute to your big life goals. Think daily lattes, subscription boxes, or impulse purchases. These are the areas where you have the most flexibility to cut back if needed.

Exercise: Expense Categorization

Look at your spending over the past month and categorize each expense into one of these three buckets. You can use your bank statements, credit card bills, or a budgeting app to help with this.

Tech Tool Spotlight: Mint
Mint is a free budgeting app that automatically categorizes your expenses. It connects to your bank accounts and credit cards, pulling in transaction data in real-time. You can customize categories to align with your values-based spending plan. Mint also offers insights into your spending patterns and sends alerts when you're approaching budget limits.

For example, Mint might show you that you're spending $200 a month on subscription services you rarely use. This could be an opportunity to redirect that money towards something more aligned with your values, like a cooking class or a savings fund for a family vacation.

As you categorize your expenses, you might have some "aha" moments. Maybe you realize you're spending a lot on things that don't really align with your values, or that you're not allocating enough to the things that do matter to you. That's okay – awareness is the first step to change!

Step 3: Implement the 50/30/20 Rule... with a Tech-Savvy Twist

You might have heard of the 50/30/20 budgeting rule before. It suggests allocating 50% of your income to needs, 30% to wants, and 20% to savings and debt repayment. We're going to put a mindful spending twist on this:

50% Essential Expenses
30% Important Expenses (aligned with your values and goals)
20% Savings/Debt Repayment

The twist? We're going to try to minimize the "Optional" category as much as possible. Any money saved from reducing optional expenses can be redirected to your Important category or to savings.

This doesn't mean you can never buy anything fun or spontaneous. The goal is to be more intentional about these purchases and to make sure they're not crowding out the things that truly matter to you.

Tech Tool Spotlight: YNAB (You Need A Budget)
YNAB is a powerful budgeting app that follows the zero-based budgeting method. It encourages you to give every dollar a job, aligning perfectly with our mindful spending approach. YNAB offers real-time syncing across devices, goal tracking, and detailed reports. While it has a learning curve, its robust features make it ideal for those serious about mindful spending.

YNAB can help you visualize how redirecting money from optional expenses to important ones or savings can impact your long-term goals. For instance, it might show you that cutting back $100 a month on dining out could allow you to fully fund your emergency savings in six months instead of a year.

Exercise: Create Your Tech-Enabled Mindful Spending Plan

Based on your expense categorization and the 50/30/20 rule, create a spending plan for the next month. Remember, this is a guideline, not a strict budget. The goal is to align your spending with your values and goals, not to make you feel restricted or deprived.

Here's an example of what this might look like:

Essential (50%):
- Rent: $1000
- Utilities: $150
- Groceries: $400
- Health Insurance: $200
- Phone/Internet: $100

Important (30%):
- Gym Membership: $50
- Online Course: $100
- Savings for Travel: $200
- Donations: $100
- Hobby Supplies: $100

Savings/Debt Repayment (20%):
- Emergency Fund: $200

- Retirement Contribution: $300

Total: $2900 (assuming a monthly take-home pay of $2900)

Remember, your plan will look different based on your income, location, and personal values and goals. The key is to make sure your spending reflects what truly matters to you.

Leveraging Technology for Conscious Consumption

Now that we have our mindful spending plan in place, let's talk about how we can use technology to support our goals. In the age of fintech, there are countless apps and tools designed to help us manage our money better. Here are some ways to leverage technology for more mindful spending:

1. Budgeting and Expense Tracking Apps

Apps like Mint, *YNAB (You Need A Budget)*, or Personal Capital can help you track your spending in real-time and categorize your expenses. Many of these apps allow you to set spending limits for different categories and will send you alerts when you're approaching your limits.

These apps can be particularly helpful in identifying patterns in your spending that you might not notice otherwise. For example, you might realize that you tend to overspend on weekends or when you're stressed. This awareness can help you develop strategies to combat these tendencies.

Pro Tip: Choose an app that allows you to customize categories to align with your values-based spending plan. This way, you can easily see how much you're spending on things that truly matter to you.

2. AI-Powered Spending Analysis

Some banks and fintech companies are now offering AI-powered insights into your spending patterns. For example, Bank of America's Erica or Cleo can analyze your transactions and provide personalized advice on where you might be overspending or how you could save more.

These AI assistants can offer a fresh perspective on your finances, pointing out things you might have missed. For instance, they might notice that you're paying for multiple streaming services with overlapping content, suggesting an opportunity to cut back.

Tech Tool Spotlight: Cleo
Cleo is an AI-powered budgeting assistant that communicates with you via text messages. It can provide witty, sometimes sassy feedback on your spending habits, making budgeting more engaging and fun. Cleo can also help you set aside money automatically and offers an interest-free salary advance feature for emergencies.

Cleo might send you a message like, "You've spent $50 on late-night snacks this week. Are you feeding a gremlin I don't know about?" This humorous approach can make you more aware of unconscious spending habits.

3. Mindful Shopping Extensions

Browser extensions like Icebox for Chrome can help curb impulse purchases by adding a "cooling off" period to your online shopping. When you click "buy," it instead adds the item to a wishlist and reminds you about it later, giving you time to consider whether it's a mindful purchase.

This digital "pause button" can be incredibly effective in reducing impulse buys. You might find that after 24 hours, you no longer feel the urge to buy that item that seemed so essential in the moment.

4. Automated Savings Apps

Apps like Acorns or Digit can help you save money without even thinking about it. They round up your purchases to the nearest dollar and invest the difference, or analyze your spending patterns to automatically transfer small amounts to savings.

These apps make saving effortless and can help you build up your emergency fund or save for specific goals without feeling the pinch in your daily life.

Tech Tool Spotlight: Acorns
Acorns is a micro-investing app that rounds up your purchases to the nearest dollar and invests the difference. For example, if you spend $3.50 on coffee, Acorns will round it up to $4 and invest the $0.50. Over time, these small amounts can add up significantly. Acorns also offers educational content to help you learn about investing.

The beauty of Acorns is that it turns everyday purchases into investment opportunities. You might be surprised at how quickly these small roundups can grow, especially when invested in a diversified portfolio.

5. Cashback and Coupon Apps

While we want to be mindful about our spending, we also want to make sure we're getting the best value when we do spend. Apps like Rakuten or Honey can automatically find and apply coupons or cashback offers for your online purchases.

These apps can help you save money on purchases you were going to make anyway, freeing up more funds for your important expenses or savings goals.

6. Subscription Tracking Apps

It's easy to lose track of all those monthly subscriptions. Apps like Truebill or Bobby can help you identify and manage your subscriptions, making it easier to cut those that don't align with your values or bring you joy.

You might be surprised to find subscriptions you forgot you had or realize that you're paying for services you rarely use. These apps make it easy to see the cumulative impact of these small monthly charges.

Tech Tool Spotlight: Truebill
Truebill not only helps you track and manage subscriptions but also negotiates bills on your behalf. It can identify recurring charges, cancel unwanted subscriptions, and even negotiate lower rates for services like cable, internet, and phone bills. This can lead to significant savings over time.

For example, Truebill might discover that you're paying for a premium cable package you rarely use and offer to negotiate a better rate or help you switch to a more suitable plan.

Exercise: Tech Tool Implementation

Choose one or two of these tech tools to implement this week. Set them up and commit to using them consistently for at least a month. At the end of the month, evaluate how they've impacted your spending habits.

Remember, these tools are meant to support your mindful spending journey, not replace your own decision-making. Use them as aids to help you stay aware and intentional about your spending.

Mindful Spending in Practice: Real-Life Scenarios

Now that we've covered the basics of mindful spending and some tools to help us, let's look at how this might play out in real-life scenarios.

Scenario 1: The Coffee Conundrum

Meet Alex, a 28-year-old marketing professional who loves her daily latte from the trendy coffee shop down the street. At $5 a pop, five days a week, that's $100 a month on coffee shop visits.

Mindless Approach: Continue the daily coffee shop habit without thinking about it.

Mindful Approach: Alex reflects on why she enjoys these coffee shop visits. Is it the caffeine boost? The ritual? The social aspect of chatting with the baristas? She realizes it's mostly about the ritual and having a special treat to look forward to.

Tech-Savvy Mindful Solution: Alex decides to limit coffee shop visits to twice a week, making them more special. She invests in a smart coffee maker that she can control with her phone, allowing her to wake up to freshly brewed coffee. She uses a recipe app to recreate her favorite latte at home. She puts the $60 saved each month towards her travel fund using an automated savings app, aligning with her value of experiencing new cultures.

By making this change, Alex doesn't feel deprived. Instead, she's created a new morning ritual at home and made her coffee shop visits more meaningful. Plus, she's actively saving for a goal that truly excites her.

Scenario 2: The Subscription Spiral

Jake, a 35-year-old teacher, realizes he's subscribed to seven different streaming services, three meal kit deliveries, two fitness apps, and a monthly box of Japanese snacks. He's spending over $200 a month on subscriptions, many of which he barely uses.

Mindless Approach: Continue all subscriptions because canceling seems like a hassle.

Mindful Approach: Jake reviews each subscription and considers how much value and joy it brings him. He also reflects on his goals of paying off student loans and spending more time outdoors.

Tech-Savvy Mindful Solution: Jake uses Truebill to identify all his subscriptions and their costs. He cancels four streaming services, keeps one meal kit delivery for busy weeks, chooses one fitness app, and decides to try making his own Japanese snacks as a fun weekend activity. He uses the Mint app to create a debt payoff plan for his student loans and sets up automatic extra payments. He also uses AllTrails, a hiking app, to find nearby trails, aligning with his goal of spending more time outdoors. The $150 saved each month is automatically split between his student loan payments and a savings account for camping equipment.

This solution allows Jake to cut unnecessary expenses without feeling deprived. He's replaced passive consumption with active hobbies that align with his values, and he's making progress on his financial goals.

Scenario 3: The Fashion Frenzy

Mia, a 31-year-old software developer, finds herself constantly buying new clothes. She loves staying on trend and the thrill of having something new, but her closet is overflowing and she's running out of storage space.

Mindless Approach: Continue buying new clothes whenever the mood strikes or a sale email lands in her inbox.

Mindful Approach: Mia reflects on why she enjoys buying new clothes and how it aligns with her values. She realizes that while she values self-expression through fashion, she also cares deeply about sustainability and reducing waste.

Tech-Savvy Mindful Solution: Mia installs the Icebox Chrome extension to add a "cooling off" period to her online shopping. She also starts using the Stylebook app to catalog her existing wardrobe and create new outfits from clothes she already owns. For when she does want something new, she downloads Depop and Poshmark to shop second-hand. She sets up a separate savings account in her banking app for clothing purchases and only buys new items when she has money in this account. The money saved goes towards her goal of taking a sustainable fashion design course, which she finds on Coursera.

By taking this approach, Mia satisfies her love for fashion while aligning her spending with her values of sustainability. She's also investing in her personal development, which could lead to new career opportunities in the future.

These scenarios illustrate how mindful spending isn't about deprivation – it's about making intentional choices that align with our values and goals. It's about questioning our habits and finding creative, tech-savvy solutions that satisfy our needs and wants while supporting our bigger life objectives.

The Environmental Impact of Mindful Consumption

As we become more mindful about our spending, it's important to consider the broader impact of our consumption habits, particularly on the environment. Mindful spending often naturally leads to reduced consumption, which can have significant positive effects on our planet.

1. Reduced Waste

When we buy less, we produce less waste. This includes not just the products themselves, but also packaging materials. By being more intentional about our purchases, we can significantly reduce the amount of waste we generate.

For example, by choosing to repair items instead of replacing them, or by opting for products with minimal packaging, we can dramatically reduce our personal waste footprint. The average American generates about 4.9 pounds of waste per day. Imagine if mindful consumption could reduce that by even 20% - that's nearly a pound less waste per person, per day!

Tech Tool Spotlight: Think Dirty
This app allows you to scan product barcodes to get information about the ingredients and their potential environmental impact. It's particularly useful for personal care and household products.

By using apps like Think Dirty, you can make more informed choices about the products you buy, considering not just their immediate use but also their long-term impact on the environment.

2. Lower Carbon Footprint
Many of our purchases, especially fast fashion and electronics, have a significant carbon footprint associated with their production and transportation. By consuming less and choosing more durable, high-quality items, we can reduce our personal carbon footprint.

For instance, the fashion industry is responsible for about 10% of global carbon emissions. By buying fewer, higher-quality clothes and wearing them for longer, we can significantly reduce our fashion-related carbon footprint.

3. Support for Sustainable Practices
Mindful spending often leads us to research and choose companies with sustainable practices. This "vote with your

dollar" approach can encourage more businesses to adopt environmentally friendly policies.

For example, by choosing to buy from B Corporations (companies certified for their social and environmental performance) or other sustainably-minded businesses, we're sending a clear message about what we value as consumers.

Tech Tool Spotlight: Good On You
This app rates fashion brands based on their impact on people, the planet, and animals. It can help you make more informed decisions when shopping for clothes, ensuring your fashion choices align with your values.

4. Conservation of Natural Resources
Every product we buy requires natural resources to produce. By consuming less, we're indirectly contributing to the conservation of these resources. This is particularly important for non-renewable resources.

For instance, the production of a single smartphone requires about 34 kg of ore to be mined. By keeping our phones for longer or buying refurbished models, we can help reduce the demand for these resources.

5. Reduction in Plastic Pollution

Mindful consumption often leads to more conscious choices about packaging and single-use plastics. This can help reduce the amount of plastic pollution entering our oceans and ecosystems.

For example, by choosing to use a reusable water bottle instead of buying bottled water, you could prevent hundreds of plastic bottles from entering the waste stream each year.

Exercise: Environmental Impact Audit
For one week, keep track of all the waste you generate from your purchases. This includes packaging, food waste, and any items you discard. At the end of the week, analyze your waste and identify areas where you can make more environmentally friendly choices.

The Psychology of Spending

Understanding the psychological factors that influence our spending habits is crucial for developing mindful consumption practices. Let's explore some key concepts:

a) The Hedonic Treadmill
This psychological phenomenon suggests that humans quickly return to a relatively stable level of happiness

despite major positive or negative events. In the context of spending, it means that the joy we get from new purchases is often short-lived, leading to a cycle of continuous consumption in search of happiness.

For example, you might feel a rush of excitement when you buy a new gadget, but that feeling often fades quickly, leading you to seek out the next purchase for another hit of happiness.

b) Loss Aversion
People tend to prefer avoiding losses to acquiring equivalent gains. This can lead to overspending on warranties or insurance for purchases, even when it's not financially sensible.

For instance, you might be more willing to spend $50 on an extended warranty for a $200 item, even if the likelihood of needing that warranty is low.

c) Social Comparison
The desire to keep up with peers or societal standards can drive unnecessary spending. This is often referred to as "keeping up with the Joneses."

Social media has amplified this effect, with platforms like Instagram creating constant pressure to showcase a certain lifestyle, often leading to unnecessary purchases.

d) Retail Therapy

Many people shop to alleviate negative emotions, using spending as a form of self-soothing. While this might provide temporary relief, it often leads to financial stress and clutter.

Understanding these psychological factors can help us make more mindful decisions about our spending. When you feel the urge to buy something, pause and ask yourself:

- Am I buying this to fill an emotional need?
- Will this purchase truly increase my long-term happiness?
- Am I influenced by social pressure or marketing tactics?

Tech Tool Spotlight: Cleo

This AI-powered budgeting assistant uses cognitive behavioral therapy techniques to help you understand and change your spending habits. It can provide insights into your emotional spending triggers and offer strategies to overcome them.

For example, Cleo might notice that you tend to make large purchases late at night when you're feeling stressed, and suggest alternative stress-relief activities.

Mindful Spending in the Digital Age

The rise of e-commerce and digital payment methods has made spending easier than ever. While this convenience can be beneficial, it also presents challenges for mindful spending. Here are some strategies to maintain mindfulness in the digital spending landscape:

a) Implement Digital "Cooling Off" Periods
Use browser extensions like Icebox for Chrome to add a pause between seeing an item online and purchasing it. This can help reduce impulse buys.

For instance, you might set a 24-hour cooling off period for any purchase over $50. This gives you time to consider whether the item aligns with your values and financial goals.

b) Unsubscribe from Marketing Emails
Constant sales notifications can trigger unnecessary spending. Unsubscribe from retailer emails or use a service like Unroll.me to manage your subscriptions.

By reducing the number of temptations in your inbox, you're less likely to make impulse purchases based on fear of missing out (FOMO) on a good deal.

c) Use Cash for Discretionary Spending

For non-essential purchases, consider withdrawing a set amount of cash each week. This makes spending more tangible and helps you stick to a budget.

Studies have shown that people tend to spend less when using cash compared to credit cards, likely because parting with physical money feels more "real" than swiping a card.

d) Practice Mindful Scrolling

Be aware of how social media influences your desire to spend. Unfollow accounts that trigger unhealthy spending habits and seek out content that aligns with your financial goals.

Consider following personal finance experts or minimalist lifestyle accounts instead of influencers who promote constant consumption.

Tech Tool Spotlight: Freedom
This app allows you to block distracting websites and apps across all your devices. You can use it to limit access to

online shopping sites during certain hours, helping you avoid late-night impulse purchases.

Exercise: Digital Detox Challenge
Choose one day a week to disconnect from online shopping completely. Use this time to reflect on your spending habits and engage in free activities that bring you joy.

Mindful Spending and Relationships

Money is often cited as a major source of conflict in relationships. Practicing mindful spending can help foster healthier financial dynamics with partners, family, and friends.

a) Open Communication
Regularly discuss financial goals and concerns with your partner. Be honest about your spending habits and work together to create shared financial objectives.

Set aside time for regular *"money dates"* where you can review your finances together in a relaxed, non-judgmental environment.

b) Align Values

Ensure that your spending as a *couple reflects* both partners' values and priorities. This might mean compromising on certain expenses and finding creative solutions that satisfy both parties.

For example, if one partner values travel while the other prefers home improvements, you might agree to alternate your focus each year.

c) Set Boundaries

Establish *clear guidelines for individual and joint spending.* This can include agreeing on a threshold for purchases that require discussion or setting individual "fun money" allowances.

You might decide that any purchase over $200 needs to be discussed first, or that each partner gets $100 per month to spend on whatever they want, no questions asked.

d) Practice Gratitude

Regularly express appreciation for the things you already have. This can help reduce the desire for unnecessary purchases and foster contentment.

Consider starting a gratitude journal where you and your partner can each write down three things you're grateful for each day.

Tech Tool Spotlight: Honeydue
This app is designed specifically for couples to manage their finances together. It allows you to sync accounts, set budgets, and communicate about financial matters within the app.

Exercise: Money Date Night
Schedule a monthly "money date" with your partner. Use this time to review your finances, discuss upcoming expenses, and align your financial goals. Make it enjoyable by including a special treat or activity as part of the date.

Mindful Spending and Career Choices

Our approach to spending can significantly impact our career decisions. By adopting a mindful spending mindset, we can create more freedom and flexibility in our professional lives.

a) Reduce Lifestyle Inflation
As your income increases, resist the urge to automatically increase your spending. Instead, use additional income to *build savings* and invest in your future.

For example, if you get a 5% raise, consider putting 3% towards your retirement savings and 2% towards lifestyle improvements.

b) Build an Emergency Fund

Having a *robust emergency fund* can provide the security to take calculated risks in your career, such as starting a business or changing industries.

Aim to save 3-6 months of living expenses in an easily accessible savings account. This can give you the confidence to pursue new opportunities without fear of financial instability.

c) Invest in Personal Development

Allocate resources to skills and experiences that can advance your career. This might include courses, conferences, or networking events.
Consider setting aside a percentage of your income specifically for professional development. This is an investment in your future earning potential.

d) Consider the Work-Life Balance

Sometimes, a lower-paying job with better *work-life balance* can lead to greater overall well-being and reduced stress-related spending.

Remember that time is a valuable resource too. A job that allows you more free time might enable you to save money by cooking at home more often or pursuing low-cost hobbies.

Tech Tool Spotlight: LinkedIn Learning
This platform offers a wide range of professional development courses. By investing in your skills, you can increase your earning potential and job satisfaction.

Exercise: Career Cost-Benefit Analysis
List your current job-related expenses (commute, work clothes, meals, etc.). Then, calculate the true hourly rate of your job after accounting for these expenses. Use this information to make more informed decisions about your career and spending habits.

Mindful Spending and Health

Our spending habits can have a significant impact on our physical and mental health. By adopting a mindful approach to health-related expenses, we can improve our well-being while potentially reducing costs.

a) Preventive Care

Invest in regular check-ups and preventive measures. While this might seem like an added expense in the short term, it can lead to significant savings and better health outcomes in the long run.

For example, regular dental cleanings can prevent costly procedures down the line. Similarly, annual physicals can catch health issues early when they're often more treatable and less expensive to address.

b) Healthy Eating

Allocate your food budget towards nutritious, whole foods. While these might sometimes be more expensive than processed alternatives, they can lead to better health and reduced medical expenses over time.

Consider using meal planning apps to help you make the most of your grocery budget while focusing on nutritious options.

c) Exercise

Consider cost-effective ways to stay active, such as home workouts, outdoor activities, or community sports leagues. This can be more sustainable than expensive gym memberships that often go unused.

Tech tools like fitness apps or YouTube workout channels can provide guided exercises at a fraction of the cost of a gym membership.

d) Stress Management
Invest in stress-reduction techniques like meditation apps or yoga classes. Reducing stress can lead to better overall health and potentially decrease stress-induced spending.

Apps like Headspace or Calm can provide guided meditations and mindfulness exercises at a lower cost than in-person classes.

Tech Tool Spotlight: MyFitnessPal
This app helps you track your diet and exercise, making it easier to make informed decisions about your health-related spending.

Exercise: Health Spending Audit
Review your health-related expenses for the past month. Categorize them into "preventive," "reactive," and "lifestyle" expenses. Look for areas where you can shift more of your spending towards preventive measures.

The Future of Mindful Spending

As we look ahead, several trends are shaping the future of mindful spending:

a) Circular Economy

More businesses are adopting circular economy principles, designing products for longevity, repairability, and recyclability. As consumers, we can support this trend by choosing products from companies committed to sustainability.

For example, companies like Patagonia offer repair services for their products, encouraging customers to keep items longer rather than replacing them.

b) Sharing Economy

Platforms that facilitate sharing and renting items rather than owning them are becoming more prevalent. This allows for more efficient use of resources and can reduce individual spending.

Services like Rent the Runway for clothing or Turo for cars allow people to access items they need without the full cost of ownership.

c) Digital Currencies and Blockchain

These technologies have the potential to make transactions more transparent and reduce fees, potentially allowing for more mindful allocation of resources.

Cryptocurrencies and blockchain technology could revolutionize how we think about and use money, potentially leading to more conscious spending habits.

d) Artificial Intelligence in Personal Finance

AI-powered tools are becoming more sophisticated in analyzing spending patterns and providing personalized advice for mindful consumption.

In the future, AI might be able to predict our spending needs and suggest the most cost-effective and sustainable options based on our personal values and goals.

Tech Tool Spotlight: Blockchain.com
This platform allows you to manage various cryptocurrencies and learn about blockchain technology, which could play a significant role in the future of mindful spending.

Exercise: Future-Proof Your Spending

Identify one area of your spending that could be more sustainable or efficient. Research emerging technologies or services in this area and create a plan to incorporate them into your lifestyle.

Quick Start Guide: 5 Steps to Jumpstart Your Mindful Spending Journey

1. Track Your Spending: Use a budgeting app like Mint or YNAB to track all your expenses for a month. This will give you a clear picture of where your money is going.

2. Identify Your Values: Take 15 minutes to write down what truly matters to you in life. These core values will guide your spending decisions.

3. Implement a Cooling-Off Period: Install the Icebox Chrome extension to add a 24-hour delay to online purchases over $50. This helps reduce impulse buying.

4. Set Up Automated Savings: Use an app like Acorns to round up your purchases and invest the difference. This painless saving method can add up quickly.

5. Conduct a Subscription Audit: Use Truebill to identify all your recurring subscriptions. Cancel those that don't align with your values or bring you joy.

Conclusion: Your Mindful Spending Journey

As we wrap up this chapter on mastering the art of mindful spending, remember that this is a journey, not a destination. Your relationship with money and consumption will continue to evolve as your life circumstances and values change.

The key is to remain conscious and intentional about your choices, regularly reflecting on how your spending aligns with your values and goals. Here are some final tips to keep in mind:

1. Regular Check-ins: Schedule monthly "money dates" with yourself to review your spending and make sure it's aligning with your values and goals. Use this time to adjust your budget, review your progress on financial goals, and plan for upcoming expenses.

2. Stay Flexible: Life happens. Be willing to adjust your spending plan as your circumstances change. Maybe you've received a promotion, or perhaps you're facing an unexpected expense. Your mindful spending approach should be adaptable to these changes.

3. Celebrate Wins: Acknowledge and celebrate when you make mindful spending decisions, no matter how small. Did you resist an impulse purchase? Did you find a more cost-effective way to enjoy your favorite hobby? Celebrate these victories to reinforce positive habits.

4. Keep Learning: Stay curious about personal finance and keep exploring new tools and strategies for mindful money management. The financial world is constantly evolving, and there's always more to learn.

5. Share Your Journey: Don't be afraid to discuss money and mindful spending with friends and family. You might inspire others to start their own journey! Plus, having a support system can help you stay accountable to your goals.

Remember, the goal of mindful spending isn't to restrict yourself or never have fun. It's about using your money as a tool to create a life that truly reflects what matters most to you. By making conscious choices about your consumption, you're not just improving your own financial well-being – you're contributing to a more sustainable and equitable world for all.

As you move forward on your mindful spending journey, keep this quote from Henry David Thoreau in mind: "The price of anything is the amount of life you exchange for it." Make sure that exchange is always worth it.

Self-Assessment Quiz: How Mindful is Your Spending?

To help you gauge where you currently stand with your mindful spending habits, take this quick self-assessment quiz. For each statement, rate how much you agree on a scale of 1 (strongly disagree) to 5 (strongly agree):

1. I know my core values and consider them when making purchases.
2. I track my expenses regularly and know where my money is going.
3. I have a clear understanding of my needs versus my wants.
4. I rarely make impulse purchases.
5. I consider the environmental impact of my consumption habits.
6. I feel in control of my spending, rather than controlled by it.
7. I'm comfortable saying no to purchases that don't align with my values or goals.
8. I regularly review and cancel unnecessary subscriptions.
9. I use technology tools to support my mindful spending habits.

10. I feel satisfied with my current spending patterns.

Scoring:

40-50: Congratulations! You're a mindful spending master. Keep up the great work!

30-39: You're on the right track. Focus on areas where you scored lower to improve your mindful spending habits.

20-29: There's room for improvement. Consider which areas you want to work on first.

10-19: Your spending could use some more mindfulness. Don't worry – you've taken the first step by recognizing it!

Remember, this quiz is just a starting point. Use your results to identify areas where you might want to focus your mindful spending efforts.

Looking Ahead: The Ripple Effects of Mindful Spending

As we conclude this chapter, let's take a moment to imagine the potential long-term impacts of your new mindful spending habits:

1. Financial Freedom: By aligning your spending with your values and goals, you're paving the way for greater financial freedom and security. Imagine the peace of mind that comes with knowing you're in control of your finances.

2. Reduced Stress: As you gain control over your spending, you'll likely experience less financial anxiety and stress. This can have positive effects on your overall mental and physical health.

3. Increased Satisfaction: When your purchases align with your values, you're likely to feel more satisfied and fulfilled. You'll be surrounded by things that truly matter to you, rather than clutter that doesn't bring you joy.

4. Environmental Impact: Mindful consumption often leads to reduced waste and support for more sustainable products and practices. Your choices can contribute to a healthier planet.

5. Positive Influence: Your mindful approach to money may inspire friends and family to reconsider their own spending habits. You could be the catalyst for positive change in your community.

6. Personal Growth: The skills you develop through mindful spending – self-reflection, delayed gratification, aligning actions with values – can spill over into other areas of your life, leading to personal growth and increased life satisfaction.

In the next chapter, we'll build on this foundation as we explore strategies for navigating debt in the modern financial landscape. But for now, take some time to reflect on what you've learned about mindful spending and start implementing your new strategies. Remember, every mindful decision is a step towards financial mastery and overall well-being. You've got this!

Chapter 3: Navigating the Debt Maze

Welcome to the debt maze, fellow millennials and Gen Z-ers! If you're feeling like you're trapped in a financial labyrinth that would make the Minotaur jealous, you're not alone. In this chapter, we're going to equip you with the tools you need to navigate this maze and find your way to financial freedom. So grab your smartphone (let's face it, it's probably already in your hand), and let's dive in!

Understanding the Debt Landscape

Before we start our journey through the debt maze, it's crucial to understand the terrain. Not all debt is created equal, and knowing the difference can significantly impact your payoff strategy. It's like knowing the difference between a Pikachu and a Charizard in Pokémon GO – they might both be cute, but one's definitely more powerful.

Types of Debt

1. Good Debt vs. Bad Debt

You might be thinking, "Wait, there's such a thing as good debt?" Indeed there is! It's like the difference between binge-watching educational documentaries (good debt) and spending 12 hours straight watching cat videos (bad debt). Let's break it down:

Good Debt:
- Generally has lower interest rates
- Helps you generate income or increase your net worth over time
- Examples: Mortgages, student loans, small business loans

Bad Debt:
- Usually has high interest rates
- Doesn't provide long-term financial benefits
- Examples: Credit card debt, payday loans, that impulse purchase of a life-size Darth Vader statue

Now, this doesn't mean all mortgage debt is automatically "good" or all credit card debt is inherently "bad." The key is to look at the terms of the debt and how it fits into your overall financial picture.

2. Secured vs. Unsecured Debt

Another important distinction is between secured and unsecured debt:

Secured Debt:
- Backed by an asset (collateral)
- Generally has lower interest rates
- Examples: Mortgages, car loans

Unsecured Debt:
- Not backed by an asset
- Usually has higher interest rates
- Examples: Credit card debt, personal loans, medical bills

Understanding these distinctions is crucial because they can affect your repayment strategies and the potential consequences of defaulting on the debt. It's like knowing the difference between a red shell and a blue shell in Mario Kart — both can slow you down, but one is definitely more devastating.

The Emotional Weight of Debt

Before we dive into strategies for tackling debt, it's important to acknowledge the emotional toll that debt can take. Feeling overwhelmed, anxious, or even ashamed about debt is common. It's like carrying around a financial Dementor – it can suck the joy out of life if we let it.

Remember, you're not alone in this. Millions of people struggle with debt, and it doesn't define your worth as a person. You're not a bad person for having debt, just like you're not a bad person for rage-quitting a particularly difficult level in a video game (we've all been there).

Exercise: Debt Emotions Check-In
Take a moment to reflect on your feelings about your debt. Write down:
1. Three emotions you feel when you think about your debt
2. How these emotions impact your daily life
3. One positive action you can take today to start addressing your debt

Remember, acknowledging these feelings is the first step in taking control of your debt situation. It's okay to feel overwhelmed, but don't let those feelings paralyze you. We're going to work through this together, like the Avengers assembling to take on Thanos (if Thanos was a giant credit card bill).

Mapping Your Debt

Now that we understand the different types of debt and have acknowledged our emotions around it, it's time to get a clear picture of our current debt situation. Think of this as creating a map of the debt maze – we need to know where we are before we can figure out how to get where we want to go. It's like when Marauder's Map in Harry Potter – we need to see all the secret passages and hidden corners of our debt to navigate it successfully.

Exercise: Creating Your Debt Inventory

Grab a piece of paper or open a spreadsheet. For each debt you have, write down:
1. The creditor (who you owe)
2. The total amount owed
3. The interest rate
4. The minimum monthly payment
5. The due date

Here's an example of what this might look like:

Creditor	Amount Owed	Interest Rate	Min. Monthly Payment	Due Date
Credit Card A	$5,000	18.99%	$150	15th
Student Loan	$20,000	5.5%	$250	1st
Car Loan	$12,000	4.5%	$300	20th
Medical Bill	$1,500	0%	$100	10th

Tech Tool Spotlight: Mint

Mint is a free budgeting app that can help you create this debt inventory automatically. It connects to your various accounts and can categorize your debts, making it easier to get a comprehensive view of your debt situation. It's like having JARVIS from Iron Man managing your finances – minus the British accent and ability to power a super suit.

Once you have this inventory, take a moment to calculate your total debt. This number might be scary, but remember – knowledge is power. Now that we know what we're dealing with, we can start formulating a plan to tackle it. It's like when the Avengers finally understood the full scope of Thanos' plan – scary, but necessary to start fighting back.

Debt Payoff Strategies

Now that we have our debt map, it's time to choose our path through the maze. There are several popular debt payoff strategies, each with its own pros and cons. Let's explore them:

1. The Debt Snowball Method

Made famous by financial guru Dave Ramsey, the debt snowball method focuses on paying off your smallest debts first, regardless of interest rate. Here's how it works:

1. List your debts from smallest to largest.
2. Make minimum payments on all debts except the smallest.
3. Put any extra money towards the smallest debt.
4. Once the smallest debt is paid off, move to the next smallest.

Pros:
- Quick wins can provide psychological motivation
- Simplifies the debt payoff process

Cons:
- May pay more in interest over time compared to other methods

The debt snowball method is particularly effective for those who need motivation to stick with their debt payoff plan.

Those small wins can provide the momentum you need to tackle larger debts. It's like leveling up in a video game – each small debt you pay off is like gaining XP, making you stronger for the bigger battles ahead.

2. The Debt Avalanche Method

The debt avalanche method prioritizes paying off debts with the highest interest rates first. Here's how it works:

1. List your debts from highest interest rate to lowest.
2. Make minimum payments on all debts except the one with the highest interest rate.
3. Put any extra money towards the highest-interest debt.
4. Once the highest-interest debt is paid off, move to the next highest.

Pros:
- Saves the most money in interest over time
- Mathematically the most efficient method

Cons:
- May take longer to see progress, which can be demotivating for some

The debt avalanche method is ideal for those who are motivated by logic and want to minimize the total amount they pay over time. It's like choosing to fight the boss monster first in a video game – it's tougher at the start, but it makes the rest of the game easier.

Tech Tool Spotlight: Undebt.it
Undebt.it is a free web app that allows you to input your debts and compare different payoff methods. It can show you exactly how much you'll save and how long it will take to become debt-free using each method. It's like having a financial time machine, showing you different possible futures based on your debt payoff choices.

3. The Debt Consolidation Method

Debt consolidation involves combining multiple debts into a single loan or credit card, ideally with a lower interest rate. This can be done through:

- Balance transfer credit cards
- Personal loans
- Home equity loans or lines of credit (for homeowners)

Pros:
- Can lower overall interest rate
- Simplifies payments (one payment instead of many)

Cons:
- May require good credit to qualify for the best rates
- Potential for fees (e.g., balance transfer fees)
- Risk of running up new debt on paid-off credit cards

Debt consolidation can be a powerful tool, but it's crucial to address the underlying spending habits that led to the debt in the first place. Otherwise, you might find yourself back in debt with an additional consolidation loan to pay off. It's like using the Infinity Gauntlet to snap away your debt – powerful, but dangerous if you don't change your habits.

4. The Debt Snowflaking Method

The debt snowflaking method involves making small, extra payments towards your debt whenever possible. It can be combined with other methods like the snowball or avalanche. Here's how it works:

1. Choose your main debt payoff strategy (e.g., snowball or avalanche).
2. Look for small amounts of money you can put towards debt:
   - Found $5 in your coat pocket? Put it towards debt.

- Got a $20 rebate? Debt payment.
- Skipped your daily latte? That $4 goes to debt.

Pros:
- Makes debt payoff feel more manageable
- Helps create a habit of prioritizing debt payoff
- Can significantly speed up debt repayment over time

Cons:
- Requires consistent effort and mindfulness
- May be harder to track

The debt snowflaking method is great for those who want to make debt payoff a daily habit and are motivated by seeing constant progress, even if it's small. It's like collecting coins in a video game – each small amount adds up over time to something significant.

Tech Tool Spotlight: Qoins
Qoins is an app that automates the debt snowflaking process. It rounds up your purchases to the nearest dollar and applies the difference to your debt. For example, if you spend $3.50 on coffee, it rounds up to $4 and puts $0.50 towards your debt. It's like having a piggy bank that automatically sends its contents to your creditors.

Choosing Your Debt Payoff Strategy

Now that we've explored different debt payoff strategies, how do you choose the right one for you? Consider these factors:

1. *Your personality and motivation style*
   - Do you need quick wins to stay motivated, or are you driven by logic and efficiency?

2. *Your financial situation*
   - How much extra money do you have to put towards debt each month?
   - What are the interest rates on your debts?

3. *Your timeline*
   - How quickly do you want to be debt-free?

4. *Your other financial goals*
   - Are you also trying to save for emergencies or invest for retirement?

Remember, there's no one-size-fits-all approach to debt payoff. You might even decide to combine methods – for example, using the snowball method for small debts while tackling your highest-interest debt avalanche-style. It's like creating your own unique character build in an RPG – you can mix and match strategies to fit your personal style and goals.

Exercise: Debt Payoff Strategy Selection

Based on what you've learned, which debt payoff strategy appeals to you most? Write down:
1. Your chosen strategy (or combination of strategies)
2. Why you think this strategy will work best for you
3. Any potential challenges you foresee in implementing this strategy
4. How you plan to overcome these challenges

Negotiating with Creditors

Before we dive deeper into implementing your chosen debt payoff strategy, let's talk about a powerful tool in your debt-fighting arsenal: negotiation. Many people don't realize that it's often possible to negotiate with creditors for better terms. It's like haggling at a bazaar, except instead of rugs and spices, you're bargaining over interest rates and payment terms.

Here's how:

1. Lower Interest Rates

For credit card debt, simply calling your credit card company and asking for a lower interest rate can be surprisingly effective. Here's a script you can use:

"Hello, I've been a loyal customer for [X] years and have always made my payments on time. However, I've recently received offers from other credit cards with lower interest rates. I'd like to keep my account with you, but the high interest rate is making me consider a balance transfer. Is there any way you could lower my interest rate?"

It's like asking for a student discount – the worst they can say is no, but you might be surprised at how often they say yes.

2. Waiving Fees

If you've incurred a late fee or over-limit fee, especially if it's your first time, many creditors will waive it if you ask. Try this script:

"I noticed a [late fee/over-limit fee] on my last statement. I've been a good customer and this is my first time [being late/going over the limit]. Would you be willing to waive this fee as a one-time courtesy?"

It's like asking your professor for an extension on a paper — if you've been a good student overall, they're often willing to cut you some slack.

3. Hardship Programs

If you're experiencing financial hardship (job loss, medical issues, etc.), many creditors offer hardship programs that can temporarily lower your interest rate or payments. Be honest about your situation and ask what options are available.

4. Debt Settlement

For debts that you're struggling to pay, especially if they're in collections, you might be able to negotiate a lump-sum settlement for less than you owe. This should generally be a last resort, as it can negatively impact your credit score.

Remember, the worst they can say is no. Be polite but persistent, and don't be afraid to ask to speak to a supervisor if the first person you talk to can't help. It's like trying to get past a bouncer at an exclusive club —

sometimes you need to talk to the manager to get what you want.

Tech Tool Spotlight: Trim

Trim is a financial assistant app that can negotiate with your creditors on your behalf. It can help lower your bills and cancel subscriptions you no longer need, freeing up more money for debt payoff. It's like having a financial bodyguard, fighting for your financial interests.

Implementing Your Debt Payoff Plan

Now that we've chosen our strategy and explored negotiation tactics, it's time to put our plan into action. Here's a step-by-step guide to implementing your debt payoff plan:

Step 1: Create a Debt Payoff Budget

Review your current budget (or create one if you haven't already) and identify areas where you can cut back to free up more money for debt payoff. Remember the mindful spending techniques we discussed in Chapter 2!

Exercise: Debt Payoff Budget Creation

1. List all your monthly income sources
2. List all your monthly expenses

3. Identify non-essential expenses you can reduce or eliminate

4. Calculate how much extra you can put towards debt each month

It's like Marie Kondo-ing your finances – keep the expenses that spark joy (or are necessary), and thank the rest for their service before letting them go.

Step 2: Set Up Your Debt Payoff System

Based on your chosen strategy (snowball, avalanche, etc.), organize your debts in the order you'll pay them off.

Tech Tool Spotlight: Debt Payoff Planner
This app allows you to input your debts and choose your payoff strategy. It then creates a payoff plan and shows you exactly when you'll be debt-free if you stick to the plan. It's like having a GPS for your debt journey, showing you the fastest route to financial freedom.

Step 3: Automate Your Payments
Set up automatic payments for at least the minimum payment on all your debts. This ensures you never miss a payment and incur late fees.

Step 4: Apply Extra Payments

Any extra money you've identified in your budget should go towards the debt you're focusing on based on your chosen strategy.

Step 5: Track Your Progress

Regularly update your debt tracker to see how much progress you're making. Celebrate your wins, no matter how small!

Exercise: Debt-Free Date Calculation

Use a debt payoff calculator (many are available online for free) to determine your debt-free date based on your current plan. Write this date down and put it somewhere you'll see it often as motivation. It's like having a countdown to your financial Independence Day!

Overcoming Debt Payoff Challenges

As you embark on your debt payoff journey, you're likely to encounter some challenges. Let's address some common ones and how to overcome them:

1. Unexpected Expenses

Life has a way of throwing financial curveballs when we least expect them. It's like you're in the middle of a game of financial Quidditch, and suddenly a Bludger comes out of nowhere!

To prepare:
- Build an emergency fund alongside your debt payoff efforts. Even a small cushion of $500-$1000 can help absorb minor shocks.
- Consider keeping a 0% APR credit card for true emergencies (but be disciplined about using it). It's like having a Time-Turner for your finances – use it wisely!

Tech Tool Spotlight: Digit
Digit is an app that analyzes your spending patterns and automatically saves small amounts of money you won't miss. It's like having a financial Dobby, quietly saving money for you in the background.

2. Debt Fatigue

Paying off debt can be a long process, and it's normal to feel tired or discouraged at times. It's like you're on a financial version of "The Long Way Up" – the journey is tough, but the destination is worth it.

To combat this:

- Celebrate small milestones along the way. Did you pay off $500? That's worth a (budget-friendly) celebration!
- Visualize your debt-free life regularly. Create a vision board or use an app like Dreamboard to keep your goals front and center.
- Connect with others on similar journeys for support and motivation. Join online communities like r/personalfinance or find local meetups.

3. Lifestyle Creep

As you get better at managing your money, you might be tempted to increase your spending. It's like leveling up in a game and immediately spending all your coins on cosmetic upgrades.

Remember:

- Stay focused on your long-term financial goals. That designer bag can wait until you're debt-free.
- Find free or low-cost ways to reward yourself for progress. A picnic in the park can be just as rewarding as an expensive dinner out.

- Remind yourself why becoming debt-free is important to you. Keep your "why" visible – maybe as your phone wallpaper?

4. Multiple Financial Goals

You might be trying to save for retirement or other goals while paying off debt. It's like trying to juggle flaming torches while riding a unicycle – tricky, but not impossible!

To balance this:
- Prioritize high-interest debt payoff. It's usually the smartest financial move.
- Consider the psychological benefits of making at least small contributions to other goals. Even $20 a month towards retirement can help you feel like you're making progress.
- Reassess and adjust your strategy regularly. Your financial journey isn't a straight line – be prepared to zigzag.

Tech Tool Spotlight: You Need A Budget (YNAB)
YNAB is a budgeting app that can help you manage multiple financial goals simultaneously. It encourages you to "give every dollar a job," which can help you balance debt payoff with other financial priorities. It's like having a financial

Sorting Hat, helping you allocate your money to where it needs to go.

Building Your Support System

Navigating the debt maze can feel overwhelming, but you don't have to do it alone. Building a support system can be crucial for staying motivated and on track. Whether it's through digital communities, professional advisors, or personal networks, having people around you who understand your goals can make all the difference.

1. Digital Communities

The internet is full of supportive communities where people share their debt-free journeys, tips, and encouragement. These online spaces can provide accountability and motivation when you're feeling stuck.

- Reddit's r/personalfinance: This subreddit is a treasure trove of advice on everything from budgeting to debt repayment strategies.
- Facebook Groups: There are numerous groups dedicated to debt reduction and financial independence where you can ask questions and share your progress.

- Instagram Accounts: Follow influencers who focus on financial wellness and debt-free living for daily inspiration.

2. Professional Support

Sometimes, you need more than just peer support—you need professional guidance. Here are some options:

- Financial Advisors: A certified financial planner (CFP) can help you create a personalized debt repayment plan.
- Credit Counselors: Non-profit credit counseling agencies offer free or low-cost services to help you manage debt.
- Debt Settlement Specialists: In extreme cases, a debt settlement company can negotiate with creditors on your behalf to reduce what you owe.

3. Personal Network

Don't underestimate the power of your personal network. Whether it's a family member who's been through a similar situation or a close friend who's great at budgeting, having someone to talk to about your financial goals can provide emotional support and practical advice. Exercise: Build Your Debt-Free Support Team

Write down three people or groups who could be part of your support team. This could include:

1. A digital community you want to join
2. A financial advisor or credit counselor
3. A trusted friend or family member

The Role of Credit Scores in Debt Management

As you work on paying off your debt, it's important to understand how this process affects (and is affected by) your credit score. Your credit score is a numerical representation of your creditworthiness, typically ranging from 300 to 850. It's like your financial GPA – a quick way for lenders to assess your credit health.

Here's what you need to know:
1. Payment History (35% of your FICO score)
   - Consistently making on-time payments is the single most important factor in improving your credit score.
   - Even one late payment can significantly impact your score, so set up automatic payments if possible.

2. *Credit Utilization (30% of your FICO score)*
   - This is the amount of credit you're using compared to your credit limits. Aim to keep this below 30%, ideally below 10%.

- As you pay down credit card balances, you'll likely see your score improve.

3. Length of Credit History (15% of your FICO score)
- The longer you've had credit accounts open, the better.
- Think twice before closing old accounts, even after paying them off. It's like keeping your old Hogwarts textbooks – they might come in handy!

4. Credit Mix (10% of your FICO score)
- Having a mix of different types of credit (credit cards, installment loans, etc.) can positively impact your score.
- Don't open new accounts just for this reason, but it's good to know if you're considering different types of credit.

5. New Credit (10% of your FICO score)
- Opening several new credit accounts in a short period can negatively impact your score.
- Each hard inquiry can slightly lower your score, so apply for new credit sparingly.

As you pay off debt, you'll likely see your credit score improve over time. However, be aware that some actions, like closing old credit card accounts, can temporarily lower your score. It's like a game of financial Jenga – each move can affect the overall structure.

Tech Tool Spotlight: Credit Karma
Credit Karma is a free service that provides regular updates on your credit score and credit report. It also offers personalized recommendations for improving your credit and alerts you to any significant changes in your credit profile. It's like having a credit score crystal ball!

Understanding how your debt payoff journey affects your credit score can help you make informed decisions and set realistic expectations. Remember, a temporary dip in your credit score is often worth the long-term benefits of becoming debt-free.

The Psychology of Debt

As we navigate the debt maze, it's crucial to understand the psychological factors that can impact our debt payoff journey. Debt isn't just a financial issue – it can have profound effects on our mental health and overall well-being. It's like carrying around a financial Dementor – it can suck the joy out of life if we let it.

1. The Debt Shame Spiral

Many people feel ashamed or embarrassed about their debt, which can lead to a cycle of avoidance and further financial problems. This "debt shame spiral" can look like:

- Avoiding opening bills or checking account balances
- Hiding debt from family or partners
- Feeling paralyzed and unable to take action
- Using more credit to maintain a facade of financial stability

Breaking free from this spiral is crucial for successful debt repayment. Remember, debt is a financial situation, not a moral failing. Acknowledging your debt and taking steps to address it is a sign of strength and responsibility.

Exercise: Debt Shame Reflection

Write down any feelings of shame or embarrassment you have about your debt. Then, challenge these thoughts by writing down:
1. Three things you've learned from your debt experience
2. Two actions you're taking to improve your financial situation
3. One person you can talk to for support

2. The Ostrich Effect

Named after the myth that ostriches bury their heads in the sand when faced with danger, the Ostrich Effect in finance refers to the tendency to avoid negative financial information. It's like playing financial peek-a-boo – if you can't see it, it doesn't exist, right? (Spoiler alert: It does.)

This might manifest as:
- Not checking account balances
- Ignoring credit card statements
- Avoiding conversations about money

While it might provide temporary relief, the Ostrich Effect can lead to missed payments, accumulating interest, and worsening financial situations.

To combat this:
- Set up automatic alerts for low balances or due dates
- Schedule regular "money check-ins" with yourself
- Use apps that gamify financial management to make it less daunting

Tech Tool Spotlight: Mint
Mint can send you regular updates on your account balances, bill due dates, and unusual spending. It's like

having a financial owl delivering important messages to you regularly.

Exercise: Financial Reality Check
Set aside 30 minutes this week for a "financial check-in." Log into all of your accounts—credit cards, loans, bank accounts—and take note of where things stand:

1. How much total debt do I have?
2. What are my current balances?
3. What are my upcoming due dates?

Once you've done this, congratulate yourself! You've taken the first step toward gaining control over your finances.

3. Retail Therapy: The Emotional Side of Spending

We've all been there—feeling stressed or upset and turning to shopping as a way to cope (*hello online shopping cart!*). This phenomenon is known as "retail therapy," and while it might provide temporary relief from negative emotions, it often leads to buyer's remorse—and more debt. Why do we engage in retail therapy?

- Shopping releases dopamine—a "feel-good" chemical in our brains.
- It provides instant gratification—a quick fix for emotional discomfort.

To break the cycle:

- Practice mindfulness before making purchases. Ask yourself: "Am I buying this because I need it or because I'm trying to feel better?"
- Find alternative ways to cope with stress—exercise, journaling, or talking with friends can provide long-term emotional benefits without adding to your financial burden.

4. Decision Fatigue

Making constant decisions about budgeting, spending, and debt repayment can lead to decision fatigue, where the quality of our decisions deteriorates after a long session of decision-making. This can lead to poor financial choices or inaction. It's like trying to solve a Rubik's Cube after a marathon – your brain is just too tired to make good choices.

To combat decision fatigue:
- Automate as many financial decisions as possible (e.g., automatic payments, savings transfers)
- Make important financial decisions early in the day when your mind is fresh
- Use decision-making frameworks (like the ones we discussed earlier) to simplify choices

5. The Debt Snowball Effect on Motivation

As we discussed earlier, the debt snowball method involves paying off the smallest debts first. While this isn't always the most mathematically efficient method, it can be psychologically powerful. Each small debt paid off provides a "quick win," boosting motivation and confidence.

This psychological boost can be crucial for maintaining momentum in your debt payoff journey. It's like leveling up in a video game – each small victory gives you the energy to tackle bigger challenges.

Tech Tool Spotlight: Debt Payoff Planner
This app allows you to visualize your debt payoff journey, showing you how each payment brings you closer to your debt-free goal. This visual representation can be a powerful motivator. It's like having a financial Marauder's Map, showing you the path to financial freedom.

Debt and Relationships

Debt doesn't just affect us individually – it can have a significant impact on our relationships, particularly with romantic partners. It's like bringing a third wheel on all your dates – and not a fun one. Let's explore how to navigate debt in the context of relationships:

1. Communication is Key

Open, honest communication about debt is crucial in relationships. Hiding debt from a partner can lead to trust issues and financial problems down the line. It's like trying to hide a dragon in your backyard – eventually, it's going to make itself known, and probably not in a good way.

Here are some tips for discussing debt with a partner:

- Choose a calm, private time to have the conversation
- Be honest about the amount of debt and how it was accrued
- Focus on solutions and future plans, not blame
- Be prepared to listen to your partner's concerns and feelings

2. Merging Finances

For couples considering merging finances, debt can complicate the process. It's like trying to merge two different Spotify playlists – you need to figure out what works for both of you.

Here are some options to consider:

- Keep finances separate until debt is paid off
- Merge some accounts while keeping debt separate
- Tackle debt together as a team

There's no one-size-fits-all approach – the key is to find a solution that works for both partners and aligns with your shared financial goals.

3. Supporting a Partner with Debt

If your partner is dealing with debt, here are some ways to offer support:

- Be non-judgmental and empathetic
- Offer to help create a budget or debt repayment plan
- Suggest low-cost date ideas to support their debt payoff goals
- Celebrate their progress and milestones

Remember, supporting a partner through debt repayment is a marathon, not a sprint. Patience and understanding are key.

Debt Fatigue

Paying off debt can feel like running a marathon. You start strong, but halfway through, you might hit a wall—known as "debt fatigue." This is when the excitement of starting your debt-free journey wears off, and you begin to feel overwhelmed by how much further you have to go. It's like being stuck in a never-ending loop of *Groundhog Day*, where every day feels like you're paying bills but not making progress. To combat debt fatigue:

- Break it down: Focus on small, achievable goals. Instead of thinking about how much total debt you have, focus on paying off one credit card or loan at a time.
- Celebrate milestones: Every time you pay off a debt, no matter how small, celebrate! Treat yourself to something inexpensive but meaningful—a movie night at home or a picnic in the park.
- Visualize your progress: Use a debt repayment tracker or app that visually shows your progress. Seeing that balance go down can be incredibly motivating.

Tech Tool Spotlight: Tally

Tally is an app that helps manage your credit card payments by automating them and ensuring you're always paying the lowest possible interest rate. It consolidates your payments into one easy-to-manage monthly bill, helping you avoid late fees and reduce interest charges. Tally can be a great tool for combating debt fatigue by simplifying your payments and showing you tangible progress.

The Temptation to Spend

Let's be real: we live in a world where temptation is everywhere. Social media influencers are constantly flaunting the latest gadgets, trips, and fashion trends. It's easy to fall into the trap of thinking, "I deserve this," especially when you're working hard to pay off debt. But remember, giving in to temptation now could set back your progress. To resist temptation:

- Unsubscribe from marketing emails: Those daily sale notifications are designed to make you spend impulsively. Unsubscribe from retailer emails or use an app like *Unroll.me* to manage your subscriptions.
- Use browser extensions: Install tools like *Icebox*, which adds a cooling-off period before making online purchases. This gives you time to think about whether you really need that item.
- Create a "wish list": Instead of buying something immediately, add it to a wish list and wait 30 days. If

you still want it after that period—and it fits within your budget—go ahead and treat yourself.

Exercise: Debt and Relationship Check-In

If you're in a relationship, schedule a "money date" with your partner. Use this time to:
1. Discuss your individual and shared financial goals
2. Review your debt repayment progress
3. Address any concerns or challenges
4. Plan a (budget-friendly) celebration for your next debt payoff milestone

Tech Tool Spotlight: Honeydue
Honeydue is an app designed specifically for couples to manage their finances together. It allows you to sync accounts, set budgets, and communicate about financial matters within the app. It's like having a financial couples counselor in your pocket!

The Environmental Impact of Debt

While we often think of debt in personal or economic terms, it's important to consider its environmental implications as well. The cycle of debt and consumption can have significant impacts on our planet. It's like the financial version of climate change – a global issue with personal roots.

1. Overconsumption and Debt

Often, debt is accrued through overconsumption – buying things we don't need with money we don't have. This leads to:
- Increased production of goods, which requires more natural resources
- More waste as we discard old items to make room for new purchases
- Higher carbon emissions from manufacturing and transportation of goods

2. The Fast Fashion Trap

The fashion industry is a prime example of how debt and environmental impact intersect. Fast fashion, often fueled by credit card debt, leads to:
- Excessive water usage and pollution in clothing production
- Textile waste in landfills
- Exploitation of workers in developing countries

3. Sustainable Debt Management

By managing debt responsibly and consuming mindfully, we can reduce our environmental footprint. Here's how:

- Buy quality items that last longer, reducing the need for frequent replacements
- Consider second-hand or refurbished items instead of always buying new
- Repair items when possible instead of replacing them

Tech Tool Spotlight: Good On You

This app rates fashion brands based on their ethical and environmental practices. Use it to make more sustainable clothing choices and reduce the environmental impact of your wardrobe.

Exercise: Environmental Impact Assessment

For one week, track every purchase you make. For each item, consider:

1. Do I really need this?
2. Could I borrow or rent this instead of buying?
3. What's the environmental impact of producing and disposing of this item?

At the end of the week, reflect on your consumption habits and identify areas where you can make more environmentally-friendly choices.

The Future of Debt Management

As we look towards the future, it's clear that technology will play an increasingly important role in how we manage debt. Let's explore some emerging trends and technologies that could shape the future of debt management:

1. Artificial Intelligence in Debt Counseling

AI-powered chatbots and virtual assistants are becoming more sophisticated in providing personalized debt advice. In the future, we might see:
- 24/7 AI debt counselors that can provide instant, personalized advice
- Predictive algorithms that can forecast potential debt issues before they occur
- AI-powered negotiation tools that can interact with creditors on your behalf

2. Blockchain and Decentralized Finance (DeFi)

Blockchain technology and the rise of DeFi could revolutionize lending and debt management:
- Peer-to-peer lending platforms with potentially lower interest rates
- Smart contracts that automatically adjust repayment terms based on the borrower's financial situation
- Tokenization of debt, allowing for more flexible trading and management of debt

3. Gamification of Debt Repayment

More apps and tools are likely to incorporate game-like elements to make debt repayment more engaging:
- Points, badges, and levels for reaching debt payoff milestones
- Competitive elements allowing users to compare their progress with peers
- Virtual reality experiences visualizing debt payoff progress

4. Open Banking and Financial Data Aggregation

As open banking initiatives expand, we might see:
- More accurate credit scoring based on a broader range of financial data
- Personalized debt consolidation offers based on your entire financial picture

- Easier tracking and management of debts across multiple accounts and institutions

While these trends are exciting, remember that the fundamental principles of debt management – spending less than you earn, prioritizing high-interest debt, and staying consistent with payments – will likely remain crucial regardless of technological advancements.

Quick Start Guide: 5 Steps to Jumpstart Your Debt Payoff Journey

Ready to start tackling your debt? Here's a quick start guide to get you going:

1. Face the Music: Gather all your debt information and create a complete debt inventory. Knowledge is power!

2. Choose Your Weapon: Decide on a debt payoff strategy (snowball, avalanche, or a combination) that aligns with your personality and goals.

3. Trim the Fat: Review your budget and identify areas where you can cut back to free up more money for debt repayment.

4. Automate to Dominate: Set up automatic payments for at least the minimum on all your debts to avoid late fees and credit score dings.

5. Level Up Your Income: Look for ways to increase your income, even temporarily, to accelerate your debt payoff. Side hustle, anyone?

Remember, starting is often the hardest part. Take that first step, and you're already on your way to financial freedom!

Self-Assessment Quiz: Understanding Your Debt Style
Take this quiz to better understand your relationship with debt and identify areas for improvement:

1. How do you typically handle unexpected expenses?
   a) Put them on a credit card
   b) Use emergency savings
   c) Ignore them until they become urgent
   d) Borrow from family/friends

2. What's your primary motivation for paying off debt?
   a) Reducing stress and anxiety
   b) Improving credit score
   c) Saving money on interest
   d) Financial freedom

3. How would you describe your debt management style?
   a) Proactive and organized
   b) Reactive and scattered
   c) Avoidant
   d) Strategic but inconsistent

4. When making purchases, do you:
    a) Always use credit cards for rewards
    b) Stick to cash/debit
    c) Use whatever's convenient
    d) Follow a strict budget

Scoring:

Mostly A's: Credit Dependent - Focus on building emergency savings
Mostly B's: Safety First - You're on the right track
Mostly C's: Debt Avoider - Need to face financial reality
Mostly D's: Strategic Spender - Work on consistency

Quick Start Guide: 5 Steps to Debt Freedom

1. **Take Inventory (Day 1-2)**
- List all debts with balances, interest rates, and minimum payments
- Calculate your total debt
- Pull your credit report
- Use Mint or Personal Capital to automate tracking

2. **Choose Your Strategy (Day 3-4)**
- Evaluate Snowball vs. Avalanche method
- Consider debt consolidation options
- Download debt payoff apps
- Set up automatic payments

3. **Create Your Budget (Day 5-7)**
- Track all income sources
- List essential expenses
- Identify areas to cut back
- Use YNAB or EveryDollar for budgeting

4. **Build Your Emergency Fund (Week 2)**
- Open a high-yield savings account
- Set up automatic transfers
- Aim for $1,000 initially
- Use Digit or Qapital to automate savings

5. **Start Your Debt Payoff Journey (Week 3+)**
- Make minimum payments on all debts
- Apply extra money to target debt
- Track progress with visual tools
- Celebrate small wins

Tech Tools for Modern Debt Management

In today's digital age, we have more tools than ever to help us manage and eliminate debt. Let's explore some game-changing apps and technologies that can make your debt-free journey easier and more engaging.

1. AI-Powered Debt Management - Modern AI tools can help you:
- Analyze spending patterns to identify money for debt repayment
- Predict potential financial struggles before they happen
- Negotiate with creditors automatically
- Provide personalized debt repayment strategies

Tech Tool Spotlight: Charlie
Charlie is an AI-powered financial assistant that analyzes your spending and finds ways to save money for debt repayment. Think of it as having JARVIS for your finances – minus the ability to power an Iron Man suit.

2. Gamified Debt Repayment Apps
These apps turn debt repayment into an engaging experience:

- Earn points and badges for paying off debt
- Compete with friends in debt payoff challenges
- Visualize progress through interactive graphics
- Set and track milestones with rewards

Tech Tool Spotlight: Fortune City
This app turns budgeting and debt repayment into a city-building game. Each financial decision helps you build and expand your virtual city, making money management more engaging.

3. Automated Debt Repayment Tools
- Round-up apps that apply spare change to debt
- Bill negotiation services
- Automatic payment optimization
- Interest rate reduction alerts

Environmental Impact and Sustainable Debt Management

The connection between debt and environmental impact is stronger than you might think. Here's how to make your debt repayment journey more environmentally friendly:

1. Sustainable Consumption Practices

- Choose quality over quantity
- Invest in energy-efficient appliances
- Consider second-hand purchases
- Repair instead of replace

2. Digital-First Debt Management
- Go paperless with statements and bills
- Use digital payment methods
- Choose eco-friendly banking options
- Reduce transportation emissions by banking online

3. Ethical Debt Repayment
- Support environmentally responsible lenders
- Choose green credit cards
- Invest in sustainable debt consolidation options
- Consider environmental impact in financial decisions

Mindfulness and Debt Management

Incorporating mindfulness into your debt repayment journey can make it more sustainable and less stressful:

1. Mindful Spending Practices
- Practice the 24-hour rule for purchases
- Use breathing techniques before financial decisions

- Regular money meditation sessions
- Gratitude journaling for financial progress

2. Emotional Awareness
- Identify emotional spending triggers
- Develop healthy coping mechanisms
- Build a supportive financial community
- Celebrate progress mindfully

3. Holistic Financial Wellness
- Balance debt repayment with self-care
- Consider the mental health impact of financial decisions
- Practice financial self-compassion
- Maintain work-life balance while pursuing debt freedom

Creating Your Debt-Free Vision

Visualization is a powerful tool for achieving your financial goals. Let's create a compelling vision of your debt-free future:

Exercise: Debt-Free Vision Board
Create a digital or physical vision board that represents:
- Your life without debt
- Financial goals you'll pursue

- Experiences you'll have
- The person you'll become

Tech Tool Spotlight: Canva

Use Canva's vision board templates to create a digital representation of your debt-free future.

Building Your Support System

No one should navigate the debt maze alone. Here's how to build a strong support system:

1. Digital Communities
- Join online debt-free communities
- Participate in financial forums
- Follow debt-free journey social media accounts
- Connect with virtual accountability partners

2. Professional Support
- Financial advisors
- Credit counselors
- Money coaches
- Mental health professionals specializing in financial stress

3. Personal Network
- Share your journey with trusted friends
- Join local money management groups
- Find a money buddy
- Create a family support system

Conclusion: Your Path to Financial Freedom

As we wrap up this chapter, remember that becoming debt-free is a journey, not a destination. Like any good RPG, you'll face challenges, gain experience, and level up your financial skills along the way.

Your debt-free journey might not be perfect, and that's okay. What matters is that you're taking steps toward financial freedom and creating a more sustainable relationship with money.

Chapter 4: Building Your Financial Fortress

In today's unpredictable world, having a solid financial foundation is more crucial than ever. Imagine waking up one morning to find your income disrupted due to unforeseen circumstances—a job loss, a medical emergency, or even a global pandemic. How would you cope? This chapter is dedicated to helping you build a robust financial fortress through an emergency fund and a comprehensive safety net that can withstand life's unexpected challenges.

The Power of Preparedness: Why You Need a Financial Fortress

Before we dive into the specifics of building your financial fortress, let's explore why it's so crucial. Remember in Chapter 1 when we discussed rewiring your money mindset? Well, having a solid financial safety net is a key part of that positive money psychology. It's not just about having cash stashed away—it's about creating a sense of security and empowerment that permeates every aspect of your financial life.

The Psychology of Financial Security

Studies have shown that financial stress can have a significant impact on mental health. According to a 2024 survey by the American Psychological Association, money remains a top source of stress for 72% of Americans. However, having an emergency fund can dramatically reduce this stress. It's like having a financial superhero cape—you feel more confident, more in control, and better equipped to handle whatever challenges come your way.

Research from the Journal of Financial Planning found that individuals with emergency savings reported higher levels of financial satisfaction and overall life satisfaction. This psychological benefit extends beyond just having money set aside; it's about the peace of mind that comes with knowing you're prepared for the unexpected.

Real-Life Impact: Sarah's Story

Let's look at Sarah, a 32-year-old graphic designer from Chicago. When the COVID-19 pandemic hit, her freelance work dried up almost overnight. But because Sarah had diligently built up a six-month emergency fund, she was able to weather the storm without panic. She used this time to upskill, taking online courses in UX design. When the job market rebounded, Sarah landed a higher-paying position that combined her graphic design skills with her new UX knowledge. Her emergency fund didn't just keep her afloat—it became a launchpad for career growth.

Sarah's story illustrates a crucial point: an emergency fund isn't just a financial tool; it's a catalyst for opportunity. Without the stress of immediate financial pressure, Sarah was able to invest in herself and emerge from a crisis stronger than before.

Defining Your Financial Fortress: More Than Just an Emergency Fund

When we talk about building a financial fortress, we're not just talking about a basic emergency fund. We're talking about a comprehensive financial safety net that can protect you from a variety of financial shocks. Let's break down the components:

1. Emergency Fund: This is your first line of defense—readily accessible cash for unexpected expenses or income disruptions.
2. Insurance Coverage: Adequate health, life, disability, and property insurance to protect against major financial setbacks.
3. Debt Management Plan: A strategy to reduce and eliminate high-interest debt, freeing up more resources for savings and investments.
4. Income Diversification: Multiple streams of income to reduce reliance on a single source.
5. Investments: Long-term wealth-building vehicles that can potentially be tapped in extreme circumstances.

Each of these components plays a crucial role in your overall financial security. In this chapter, we'll focus primarily on building your emergency fund, but we'll touch on these other elements as well.

The Emergency Fund: Your Financial First Aid Kit

Think of your emergency fund as your financial first aid kit. Just like you wouldn't want to be caught without bandages and antiseptic when you cut yourself, you don't want to be caught without cash when life cuts you financially.

How Much Should You Save?

The traditional advice is to save 3-6 months of living expenses. But let's be real—in today's gig economy and with the lessons learned from the pandemic, many experts are now recommending 6-12 months.

Here's a simple formula to calculate your target:

1. Add up your essential monthly expenses (rent/mortgage, utilities, food, insurance, minimum debt payments)
2. Multiply that number by the number of months you want to cover (let's say 6)

For example:

Monthly Expenses: $3,000

Target Emergency Fund: $3,000 x 6 = $18,000

But remember, this is just a guideline. Your specific situation might call for more or less. Consider factors like:

1. Job stability
2. Number of income earners in your household
3. Health conditions
4. Dependents

The Reality Check: Where Most Americans Stand

Before you start feeling overwhelmed by these numbers, let's take a look at the reality of emergency savings in America. According to a 2024 Bankrate survey:

1. Nearly two-thirds of Americans (62%) feel behind on emergency savings
2. Only 20% say they have more emergency savings now than at the start of 2024
3. 33% have less emergency savings than they did at the beginning of 2024

4. 17% had no emergency savings at the start of the year and still have none

These statistics highlight a crucial point: building an emergency fund is challenging for many people. But don't let these numbers discourage you. Instead, let them motivate you to buck the trend and secure your financial future.

Where to Keep Your Emergency Fund

Your emergency fund needs to be easily accessible, but not so accessible that you're tempted to dip into it for non-emergencies. Here are some options:

1. High-Yield Savings Account: These online accounts often offer higher interest rates than traditional banks. As of 2024, some accounts are offering APYs of up to 5.25%.
2. Money Market Account: Similar to a savings account but often with check-writing privileges.
3. Cash Management Account: These accounts, offered by many fintech companies, often combine high yields with additional features like debit cards and investment options.

4. Short-Term CD Ladder: By staggering CDs with different maturity dates, you can potentially earn higher interest while maintaining some liquidity.

Remember, the goal is liquidity and safety, not high returns. Your emergency fund is insurance, not an investment.

Building Your Emergency Fund: Strategies for Success

Now that we know why we need an emergency fund and where to keep it, let's talk about how to build it. This is where the rubber meets the road, and where many people struggle. But don't worry—we've got strategies to make it happen.

1. Start Small, Think Big

If you're starting from zero, the idea of saving several months' worth of expenses can feel overwhelming. But remember what we learned about the growth mindset in Chapter 1? Apply that here. Start with a goal of saving $1,000. This "starter emergency fund" can cover many common emergencies and give you the confidence to keep going.

2. Automate Your Savings

Remember in Chapter 2 when we talked about mindful spending? One of the best ways to ensure you're "spending" on your emergency fund is to automate it. Set up an automatic transfer from your checking account to your emergency fund savings account each payday. Treat it like any other bill—non-negotiable.

3. Use Windfalls Wisely

Tax refunds, work bonuses, cash gifts—these unexpected inflows of cash are perfect for boosting your emergency fund. Consider committing 50% of any windfall to your emergency savings.

4. Declutter for Dollars

Look around your home. Chances are, you have items you no longer need that could be converted into cash. Sell unused electronics, clothing, or furniture online or at a garage sale. Every dollar counts!

5. Earn Extra Income

In today's gig economy, there are countless ways to earn extra money. Consider freelancing, tutoring, or driving for a rideshare service. Dedicate this extra income to your emergency fund.

6. Review and Reduce Expenses

Go through your budget with a fine-tooth comb. Can you cut back on subscriptions? Negotiate better rates on your bills? Even small reductions can add up over time.

7. Make It a Challenge

Turn saving into a game. Try a savings challenge, like the 52-week challenge where you save $1 the first week, $2 the second week, and so on. By the end of the year, you'll have saved $1,378!

8. Visualize Your Progress

Use a visual aid to track your progress. This could be a simple thermometer drawing you fill in as your savings grow, or a more high-tech solution like a savings tracking app. Seeing your progress can be incredibly motivating.

Real-Life Example: The Power of Persistence

Meet Alex, a 28-year-old teacher from Atlanta. When Alex first started budgeting, the idea of saving six months of expenses seemed impossible. But he started small, setting aside just $50 from each paycheck. He sold some old textbooks and electronics, adding another $300 to his fund. Slowly but surely, his emergency fund grew.

After a year, Alex had saved $3,000—not quite six months of expenses, but a solid start. Then, his car needed major repairs. Instead of panicking or reaching for a credit card, Alex was able to pay for the $2,800 repair from his emergency fund. This experience motivated Alex to redouble his efforts, and within another year, he had built his fund back up to $5,000.

Alex's story shows that building an emergency fund is not always a straight line. There may be setbacks, but the important thing is to keep going.

Beyond the Emergency Fund: Building a Comprehensive Safety Net

While an emergency fund is a crucial component of your financial fortress, it's not the only one. Let's explore other elements that can strengthen your financial security.

Insurance: Your Financial Shield

Insurance is a key part of your financial safety net. It protects you from catastrophic expenses that could otherwise wipe out your savings. Here are some key types of insurance to consider:

1. Health Insurance: This is non-negotiable. Medical bills are one of the leading causes of bankruptcy in the U.S.
2. Disability Insurance: This replaces a portion of your income if you're unable to work due to illness or injury.
3. Life Insurance: If you have dependents, life insurance ensures they're taken care of if something happens to you.
4. Property Insurance: Homeowners or renters insurance protects your biggest assets.

5. Umbrella Insurance: This provides additional liability coverage beyond what's offered by your home and auto policies.

Remember, the goal of insurance is to protect you from financial ruin, not to profit. Choose coverage levels that adequately protect you without overinsuring.

Debt Management: Fortifying Your Finances

High-interest debt is like a leak in your financial fortress. It drains away resources that could be used for saving and investing. If you have high-interest debt, consider these strategies:

1. Debt Avalanche: Focus on paying off the highest-interest debt first while making minimum payments on others.
2. Debt Consolidation: If you have good credit, you might be able to consolidate high-interest debts into a single, lower-interest loan.
3. Balance Transfer: For credit card debt, a balance transfer to a card with a 0% introductory APR can give you breathing room to pay off the debt.

Remember what we learned about debt in Chapter 3? Apply those principles here to strengthen your overall financial position.

Income Diversification: Don't Put All Your Eggs in One Basket

Relying on a single source of income is risky in today's economy. Consider ways to diversify your income:

1. Side Hustle: Use your skills to freelance or consult on the side.
2. Passive Income: Invest in dividend-paying stocks or real estate investment trusts (REITs).
3. Create Digital Products: Write an e-book or create an online course.
4. Rent Out Assets: If you have a spare room or parking space, consider renting it out.

Income diversification not only provides additional financial security but can also accelerate your savings goals.

Investments: Building Long-Term Wealth

While your emergency fund should be kept in safe, liquid accounts, your overall financial fortress should include long-term investments. These can act as a backup to your emergency fund in extreme circumstances. Consider:

1. Retirement Accounts: 401(k)s and IRAs offer tax advantages and long-term growth potential.

2. Taxable Investment Accounts: These offer more flexibility than retirement accounts.
3. Real Estate: Whether through direct ownership or REITs, real estate can provide both income and appreciation.

Remember, investments come with risk. Never invest money you can't afford to lose, and always consider your risk tolerance and time horizon.

Maintaining Your Financial Fortress

Building your financial fortress is not a one-time event—it's an ongoing process. Here are some tips for maintaining and strengthening your financial security over time:

1. Regular Reviews: At least once a year, review your emergency fund, insurance coverage, and overall financial plan. Have your expenses changed? Do you need to increase your emergency fund?
2. Rebalance Investments: If you have investments, rebalance them periodically to maintain your desired asset allocation.
3. Stay Educated: The financial world is always changing. Stay informed about new financial products, tax laws, and economic trends that might affect your strategy.

4. Adjust for Life Changes: Major life events like marriage, having children, or changing careers may necessitate adjustments to your financial fortress.
5. Replenish After Use: If you need to use your emergency fund, make it a priority to build it back up.

Common Pitfalls to Avoid

As you build and maintain your financial fortress, be aware of these common mistakes:

1. Overlooking Inflation: The purchasing power of your emergency fund can erode over time due to inflation. Consider this when setting savings goals.
2. Neglecting to Update: Your emergency fund needs may change over time. Regularly reassess to ensure you're adequately covered.
3. Using It for Non-Emergencies: Resist the temptation to dip into your emergency fund for non-essential expenses.
4. Keeping Too Much in Cash: While having an emergency fund is crucial, keeping too much in low-yield savings accounts can mean missing out on potential investment returns.
5. Forgetting to Celebrate: Building financial security is a significant achievement. Take time to acknowledge and celebrate your progress!

Leveraging Technology for Emergency Fund Management

In today's digital age, numerous apps and tools can help you build and manage your emergency fund more effectively. Here are some top picks for 2024:

1. Rocket Money (formerly Truebill): This app helps you identify and cut unnecessary expenses, freeing up more money for your emergency fund. It also offers a built-in savings feature.
2. Acorns: This micro-investing app rounds up your purchases to the nearest dollar and invests the difference. You can set up a separate emergency fund within the app.
3. Qapital: This app allows you to set savings rules based on your spending habits, making it easier to build your emergency fund without thinking about it.
4. YNAB (You Need A Budget): While primarily a budgeting app, YNAB's philosophy of giving every dollar a job can help you prioritize your emergency fund savings.
5. Digit: This app analyzes your spending habits and automatically saves small amounts that you won't miss, perfect for building an emergency fund gradually.

Remember, while these tools can be helpful, they're just that—tools. The most important factor in building your emergency fund is your commitment to financial security.

Actionable Steps: Building Your Financial Fortress

Now that we've covered the why, what, and how of building your financial fortress, let's break it down into actionable steps:

1. Calculate Your Target: Determine how much you need in your emergency fund based on your monthly expenses and personal circumstances.
2. Choose Your Account: Select a high-yield savings account or other appropriate vehicle for your emergency fund.
3. Set Up Automatic Transfers: Arrange for a portion of each paycheck to be automatically deposited into your emergency fund. Start with a percentage you're comfortable with, even if it's just 1% of your income.
4. Review Your Insurance: Assess your current insurance coverage and identify any gaps. Consider consulting with an insurance professional to ensure you're adequately protected.

5. Create a Debt Repayment Plan: If you have high-interest debt, develop a strategy to pay it off. Use the debt avalanche or snowball method, whichever motivates you more.
6. Explore Income Diversification: Identify potential sources of additional income. Could you freelance, start a side business, or monetize a hobby?
7. Educate Yourself: Commit to ongoing financial education. Set aside time each week to read financial blogs, listen to podcasts, or take online courses.
8. Track Your Progress: Use a spreadsheet or app to monitor your progress towards your emergency fund goal. Seeing your progress can be incredibly motivating.
9. Celebrate Milestones: Set intermediate goals and reward yourself when you reach them. For example, treat yourself to a nice dinner when you reach 25% of your emergency fund goal.
10. Share Your Journey: Consider finding an accountability partner or joining a financial support group to stay motivated. Sharing your goals can help you stay committed.

Real-Life Success Stories

Let's look at a few more real-life examples of individuals who have successfully built their financial fortresses:

Maria's Freelance Safety Net

Maria, a 35-year-old freelance writer from Miami, built her emergency fund over two years. She started by saving just $50 per month, gradually increasing her contributions as her income grew. When a major client unexpectedly went out of business, Maria's six-month emergency fund allowed her to cover expenses while she found new clients. This safety net prevented her from going into debt and gave her the confidence to negotiate better rates with new clients.

The Rodriguez Family's Unified Approach

The Rodriguez family—Carlos (42), Elena (39), and their two children—made building their emergency fund a family project. They created a "savings thermometer" on their refrigerator, coloring it in as their fund grew. The kids contributed by suggesting ways to save money and even donating some of their allowance. This unified approach not only built their financial fortress but also taught their children valuable lessons about financial preparedness.

Tom's Tech-Savvy Savings

Tom, a 28-year-old software developer from Seattle, leveraged technology to supercharge his emergency fund savings. He used a round-up app to automatically save the spare change from his purchases, set up automatic transfers to a high-yield savings account, and used a budgeting app to identify areas where he could cut back. Within 18 months, he had built a robust six-month emergency fund.

These stories illustrate that regardless of your situation—whether you're a freelancer, a family, or a young professional—building a financial fortress is possible with dedication and the right strategies.

Overcoming Common Obstacles

Building your financial fortress isn't always smooth sailing. Here are some common obstacles you might face and strategies to overcome them:

Obstacle 1: "I Don't Make Enough to Save"

Strategy: Start with micro-savings. Even saving $5 a week adds up over time. Look for areas where you can cut back, even if it's just reducing one takeout meal per month.

Obstacle 2: "I Keep Dipping into My Emergency Fund"

Strategy: Create a separate "buffer fund" for non-emergency expenses that aren't part of your regular budget. This can help you avoid tapping into your true emergency fund.

Obstacle 3: "I'm Overwhelmed by Debt"

Strategy: Consider the "debt snowball" method to build momentum. Start by paying off your smallest debt while making minimum payments on others. As you pay off each debt, roll that payment into the next largest debt.

Obstacle 4: "I Can't Stay Motivated"

Strategy: Visualize your goals. Create a vision board or set up visual reminders of what financial security means to you. Celebrate small wins along the way to stay motivated.

Obstacle 5: "Unexpected Expenses Keep Popping Up"

Strategy: Review your spending for the past few months to identify recurring "unexpected" expenses. Build these into your budget as sinking funds to avoid surprises.

Remember, everyone faces obstacles on their journey to financial security. The key is to stay persistent and adjust your strategies as needed.

The Psychological Benefits of a Strong Financial Fortress

Building your financial fortress isn't just about the numbers—it can have profound psychological benefits as well. Let's explore some of these benefits:

Reduced Stress and Anxiety

A study by the American Psychological Association found that money is a top source of stress for many Americans. Having a robust emergency fund can significantly reduce this financial stress, leading to improved mental health and overall well-being.

Increased Confidence and Self-Esteem

Knowing that you're prepared for financial emergencies can boost your confidence in other areas of life. You may feel more empowered to take calculated risks, such as starting a business or changing careers.

Improved Relationships

Financial stress can strain relationships. With a strong financial fortress, you're less likely to argue about money with your partner or family members, leading to healthier, more harmonious relationships.

Greater Sense of Control

In an unpredictable world, having a financial safety net gives you a greater sense of control over your life. This can lead to reduced feelings of helplessness and increased overall life satisfaction.

Enhanced Decision-Making

When you're not constantly worried about money, you're better able to make rational, long-term decisions. This can benefit not just your finances, but other areas of your life as well.

Integrating Your Financial Fortress with Overall Financial Planning

While building your emergency fund is crucial, it's important to view it as part of your overall financial plan. Here's how your financial fortress fits into the bigger picture:

1. Debt Repayment

While building your emergency fund, you should also be working on paying down high-interest debt. A common strategy is to build a starter emergency fund of $1,000, then focus on debt repayment, and finally build your full emergency fund.

2. Retirement Savings

Once you have your emergency fund in place, you can more confidently contribute to retirement accounts knowing you have a buffer for unexpected expenses.

3. Short-Term Savings Goals

Your emergency fund strategy can be applied to other short-term savings goals, like saving for a down payment on a house or a dream vacation.

4. Investment Strategy

With a solid emergency fund, you may feel more comfortable taking calculated risks in your investment portfolio, potentially leading to higher returns over time.

5. Insurance Planning

Your emergency fund works in tandem with your insurance coverage. Adequate insurance can help prevent your emergency fund from being depleted by a single catastrophic event.

Leveraging Technology for Emergency Fund Management

In today's digital age, numerous apps and tools can help you build and manage your emergency fund more effectively. Here are some top picks for 2024:

1. Rocket Money (formerly Truebill): This app helps you identify and cut unnecessary expenses, freeing up more money for your emergency fund. It also offers a built-in savings feature.
2. Acorns: This micro-investing app rounds up your purchases to the nearest dollar and invests the difference. You can set up a separate emergency fund within the app.
3. Qapital: This app allows you to set savings rules based on your spending habits, making it easier to build your emergency fund without thinking about it.
4. YNAB (You Need A Budget): While primarily a budgeting app, YNAB's philosophy of giving every

dollar a job can help you prioritize your emergency fund savings.
5. Digit: This app analyzes your spending habits and automatically saves small amounts that you won't miss, perfect for building an emergency fund gradually.

Remember, while these tools can be helpful, they're just that—tools. The most important factor in building your emergency fund is your commitment to financial security.

The Future of Emergency Funds

As we look to the future, several trends are shaping how we think about and manage emergency funds:

AI-Powered Savings

Artificial intelligence is being used to analyze spending patterns and automatically adjust savings rates. In the future, AI might be able to predict potential emergencies and adjust your savings accordingly.

Crypto-Based Emergency Funds

Some fintech companies are exploring cryptocurrency-based emergency funds. While these offer potential benefits like higher yields, they also come with increased volatility and risk.

Community Emergency Funds

Peer-to-peer lending platforms are facilitating community-based emergency funds where members pool resources. This could provide an additional layer of financial security beyond individual emergency funds.

Employer-Sponsored Emergency Savings

Some companies are offering emergency savings accounts as an employee benefit, sometimes with matching contributions. This trend could significantly boost emergency savings rates if it becomes widespread.

Holistic Financial Wellness Platforms

These platforms integrate emergency savings with other financial goals, providing a more comprehensive view of financial health. They might use AI to balance emergency savings with other financial priorities automatically.

While these innovations are exciting, remember that the core principles of emergency funds—liquidity, safety, and adequacy—remain unchanged.

Conclusion: Your Fortress, Your Future

Building your financial fortress is more than just a smart money move—it's an investment in your peace of mind and future possibilities. With a robust emergency fund and comprehensive financial safety net, you're not just preparing for the worst; you're empowering yourself to seize opportunities and live life on your own terms.

Remember, financial security is not about having a certain amount of money—it's about having the confidence to face whatever life throws your way. As you continue on your journey to financial mastery, let your growing financial fortress be a source of pride and motivation.

In the next chapter, we'll explore how to take your financial game to the next level by mastering the art of investing in the digital age. But for now, take a moment to appreciate the solid foundation you're building. Your future self will thank you!

Chapter 5: Investing in the Digital Age

Introduction: Welcome to the Investment Revolution

Picture this: You're lounging on your couch, binge-watching the latest Netflix series, when suddenly you remember you wanted to start investing. In the past, this might have meant scheduling an appointment with a financial advisor, putting on your best "adulting" outfit, and trying to decipher complex financial jargon. But welcome to 2024, where the investment world is quite literally at your fingertips!

Gone are the days when investing was a game reserved for Wall Street suits and those with deep pockets. Today, thanks to the digital revolution, anyone with a smartphone and a few spare dollars can become an investor. It's like we've gone from an exclusive country club to a public park, and everyone's invited to the picnic.

In this chapter, we're going to dive into the exciting world of digital investing. We'll explore how technology has transformed the investment landscape, making it more accessible, efficient, and, dare we say, fun. Whether you're a complete newbie or someone looking to up your investment game, buckle up because we're about to embark on a journey through the brave new world of digital investing.

The Evolution of Investing: From Ticker Tapes to TikTok

The Analog Era: When Trees Died for Stock Quotes

Let's take a quick trip down memory lane, shall we? Picture a world where:

1. Getting stock quotes meant waiting for the morning newspaper
2. Trading required a phone call to your broker (probably named Chauncey or Reginald)
3. Your portfolio updates came via snail mail quarterly statements

Sounds like a financial stone age, right? Well, that was the reality not too long ago. Investing was about as accessible as a secret underground lair, and just as mysterious.

The Digital Revolution: Democratizing Dollar Bills

Fast forward to today, and oh boy, have things changed! The digital revolution has:

1. Eliminated the need for a personal broker (sorry, Chauncey)
2. Lowered minimum investments (in some cases to just $1)
3. Provided real-time updates and instant trades

Now, anyone with a smartphone and a few spare dollars can become an investor. It's like we've gone from exclusive country club to public park, and everyone's invited to the picnic.

The Rise of Fintech: Your New Robot Overlords (But Friendly Ones)

Fintech, or financial technology, is the cool kid on the investment block. It's disrupting traditional financial services faster than you can say "blockchain." Let's break down some of the key players in this brave new world.

Robo-Advisors: The Terminator, but for Your Finances

Robo-advisors are like having a super-smart, algorithm-driven financial advisor in your pocket. They're revolutionizing investing by:

1. Automating portfolio management
2. Providing low-cost investment options
3. Offering personalized investment strategies based on your goals and risk tolerance

Popular robo-advisors like Betterment, Wealthfront, and Acorns are making investing accessible to the masses. It's like having a mini Warren Buffett in your smartphone, minus the Cherry Coke addiction.

Spotlight on Betterment

Betterment is often hailed as the pioneer of robo-advising, and for good reason. Here's why it's worth considering:

1. Low fees: Annual management fee of just 0.25% for the basic plan
2. No minimum balance: You can start investing with any amount
3. Tax-loss harvesting: Automatically minimizes your tax burden
4. Socially responsible investing options: Align your investments with your values

But remember, while robo-advisors are great for many investors, they're not a one-size-fits-all solution. If you have complex financial needs or prefer a more personal touch, you might want to consider other options.

Micro-Investing Apps: Making Mountains Out of Pennies

Remember when saving meant putting your spare change in a piggy bank? Micro-investing apps have digitized this concept, allowing you to invest your spare change from everyday purchases. Apps like Acorns and Stash are turning your latte habit into a wealth-building strategy. It's like finding money in your couch cushions, but instead of just buying more snacks, you're investing in your future.

How Acorns Works

1. Link your debit or credit card to the app
2. Make purchases as usual
3. Acorns rounds up each purchase to the nearest dollar and invests the difference
4. Your spare change is invested in a diversified portfolio of ETFs

It's a painless way to start investing, especially if you're on a tight budget. But keep in mind, while every little bit helps, you'll need to invest more than just spare change to build significant wealth over time.

Cryptocurrency Platforms: Digital Gold Rush

Unless you've been living under a rock (which, given the housing market, might not be a bad idea), you've heard of Bitcoin and other cryptocurrencies. Platforms like Coinbase and Binance have made it possible for average Joes to get in on the crypto action. It's like the Wild West of investing, complete with boom towns, outlaws, and the occasional tumbleweed.

But before you go all-in on crypto, a word of caution: This is a highly volatile market. The value of cryptocurrencies can swing wildly in a matter of hours. It's exciting, sure, but it's also risky. Only invest what you can afford to lose, and maybe don't bet your entire retirement on Dogecoin, no matter how cute that Shiba Inu is.

The Power of Information: From Insider Trading to Insider Tweeting

In the digital age, information is power, and it's available at your fingertips. Gone are the days when Wall Street insiders had all the good intel. Now, a tweet from Elon Musk can send a stock soaring (or plummeting) faster than you can say "To the moon!"

Social Media: The New Stock Ticker

Social media platforms have become unexpected players in the investment world. Here's how:

1. Twitter: Follow financial experts, CEOs, and market analysts for real-time insights.
2. Reddit: Join communities like r/wallstreetbets for crowd-sourced investment ideas (but proceed with caution – it's a jungle out there).

3. LinkedIn: Connect with industry professionals and stay updated on company news.

Remember, though, with great power comes great responsibility. Not every hot tip on social media is golden – sometimes it's just fool's gold. Always do your own research before making investment decisions.

Financial News Apps: CNBC in Your Pocket

Apps like Yahoo Finance, Bloomberg, and CNBC have made it possible to stay updated on market news 24/7. It's like having a financial news channel that fits in your pocket, minus the loud commercials and dramatic sound effects.

But here's a pro tip: While staying informed is good, obsessively checking market news can lead to emotional decision-making. Set specific times to check your investments and the news, and try to avoid making impulsive moves based on short-term market fluctuations.

Educational Platforms: Become a Wall Street Wizard

Websites and apps like Investopedia, Khan Academy, and Coursera offer free or low-cost courses on investing. You can go from "What's a stock?" to "Let me tell you about my diversified portfolio" faster than you can say "compound interest."

The Democratization of Investing: Power to the People

The digital age has torn down many of the barriers that once made investing an exclusive club. Let's explore how technology is leveling the playing field.

Fractional Shares: Slicing the Pie

Remember when buying a single share of Amazon stock cost more than your monthly rent? Fractional shares have changed the game. Now you can own a slice of high-priced stocks for as little as $1. It's like being able to buy a single M&M instead of the whole bag (but way more profitable).

Here's how it works:

1. Choose a stock you want to invest in
2. Decide how much money you want to invest
3. Buy a fraction of a share based on that amount

This means you can invest in companies like Amazon, Google, or Berkshire Hathaway without needing thousands of dollars. It's a game-changer for small investors looking to build a diversified portfolio.

Commission-Free Trading: Goodbye, Hidden Fees

Apps like Robinhood pioneered commission-free trading, and others quickly followed suit. This has made frequent trading more accessible, especially for those starting with smaller amounts. It's like going to an all-you-can-eat buffet, but for stocks (just don't overindulge – moderation is key in both eating and investing).

But remember, just because you can trade for free doesn't mean you should be making trades all the time. Frequent trading can lead to poor investment outcomes for most individual investors. Stick to a long-term strategy and avoid the temptation to become a day trader just because you can.

ETFs and Index Funds: Diversification Made Easy

Exchange-Traded Funds (ETFs) and Index Funds have made diversification simpler than ever. Instead of trying to pick individual winning stocks, you can invest in a basket of stocks with a single purchase. It's like buying a variety pack of cereal instead of individual boxes – you get a little bit of everything.

Some popular ETFs to consider:

1. SPY: Tracks the S&P 500 index
2. VTI: Provides exposure to the entire U.S. stock market
3. VXUS: Offers international stock market exposure

Remember, diversification is key to managing risk in your portfolio. Don't put all your eggs in one basket, no matter how tempting that basket might look.

The Dark Side of Digital Investing: Pitfalls to Avoid

With great power comes great responsibility, and the ease of digital investing comes with its own set of risks. Let's explore some of the potential pitfalls.

The Gamification of Investing: When Stocks Feel Like Candy Crush

Many investing apps use game-like features to keep you engaged. While this can make investing more fun, it can also lead to impulsive decisions. Remember, you're dealing with real money, not Monopoly cash.

Signs that you might be treating investing like a game:

1. You check your investment app more often than your social media
2. You make trades based on short-term price movements rather than long-term value
3. You feel a rush of excitement (or anxiety) with each trade

If this sounds like you, it might be time to take a step back and reassess your investment strategy. Investing should be boring most of the time. If it's constantly exciting, you might be taking on too much risk.

Information Overload: Drinking from the Financial Firehose

With so much information available, it's easy to get overwhelmed. This can lead to analysis paralysis or, worse, making decisions based on incomplete or misunderstood information. It's like trying to watch every show on Netflix – sometimes, less is more.

Tips for managing information overload:

1. Choose a few reliable sources of financial information and stick to them
2. Set specific times to check market news, rather than constantly refreshing your feed
3. Focus on long-term trends rather than day-to-day market movements
4. Remember that no one can predict the market with certainty – even the experts

The FOMO Factor: When Everyone's a Stock Market Genius

Social media can make it seem like everyone's getting rich quick. This can lead to Fear of Missing Out (FOMO) and risky investment decisions. Remember, people are more likely to post about their wins than their losses. For every person bragging about their crypto millions, there are plenty who lost their shirts.

How to combat FOMO:

1. Stick to your investment plan and avoid impulsive decisions
2. Remember that slow and steady often wins the race in investing

3. Don't compare your investment journey to others — everyone's financial situation is unique
4. If something sounds too good to be true, it probably is

Sustainable and Ethical Investing in the Digital Age

As Millennials and Gen Z gain more investing power, there's a growing focus on sustainable and ethical investing. The digital age has made it easier than ever to align your investments with your values.

ESG Investing: Doing Well by Doing Good

Environmental, Social, and Governance (ESG) investing has gone mainstream. Apps and platforms now offer ESG-focused portfolios and screening tools. It's like being able to invest in companies that align with your values, without having to become an investigative journalist.

Popular ESG themes include:

1. Climate change mitigation
2. Diversity and inclusion
3. Corporate governance and ethics
4. Sustainable resource management

Many robo-advisors and traditional investment platforms now offer ESG-focused portfolios. For example, Betterment offers a Socially Responsible Investing portfolio that focuses on companies with strong ESG practices.

Impact Investing: Be the Change You Want to See in the World

Digital platforms are making it easier to invest in companies and projects that aim to make a positive social or environmental impact. It's like voting with your dollars, but with the potential for financial returns.

Platforms like Swell Investing and OpenInvest allow you to invest in themes like clean water, renewable energy, or gender equality. Just remember, while making a positive impact is great, you should still consider the financial aspects of these investments.

Green Bonds and Clean Energy ETFs: Investing in a Sustainable Future

The digital age has made it easier to invest in green bonds and clean energy ETFs. You can now support the transition to a sustainable economy with just a few taps on your smartphone. It's like planting trees, but with the potential for financial growth.

Some popular clean energy ETFs include:

1. iShares Global Clean Energy ETF (ICLN)
2. Invesco Solar ETF (TAN)
3. First Trust Global Wind Energy ETF (FAN)

As with any investment, make sure to do your research and understand the risks before diving in.

The Rise of ESG Investing: Doing Well by Doing Good

Remember when investing was all about maximizing profits, no matter the cost? Well, times are changing, my friend. Enter ESG investing - the cool new kid on the block that's all about making money while making the world a better place. It's like having your cake and eating it too, but the cake is made of sustainable, ethically sourced ingredients.

What's ESG, and Why Should You Care?

ESG stands for Environmental, Social, and Governance. It's like choosing a roommate - you want someone who's clean (Environmental), gets along with others (Social), and pays their rent on time (Governance). In investment terms:

1. Environmental factors consider a company's impact on the planet
2. Social factors look at how a company treats people (employees, customers, communities)
3. Governance factors examine how a company is run

Why should you care? Well, besides potentially helping you sleep better at night knowing your money isn't funding the next ecological disaster, ESG investing has shown some promising returns. According to a 2024 BlackRock study, 81% of a globally-representative selection of sustainable indexes outperformed their parent benchmarks during the COVID-19 downturn. Not too shabby, right?

How Digital Tools are Democratizing ESG Investing

1. ESG Ratings and Screeners: Many investment apps now offer ESG ratings for stocks and funds. It's like having a sustainability report card for your investments right at your fingertips.
2. Robo-Advisors with ESG Focus: Some robo-advisors now offer ESG-focused portfolios. It's like having a robot assistant that not only manages your money but also shares your values.
3. ESG ETFs: Exchange-Traded Funds focusing on ESG criteria have proliferated. These allow you to

invest in a basket of ESG-friendly companies with a single purchase.

4. AI-Powered ESG Analysis: Artificial Intelligence is being used to analyze vast amounts of data to assess companies' ESG performance. It's like having a super-smart sustainability expert working 24/7 to evaluate your investments.

Real-Life Example: The Rise of Sustainable Robo-Advisors

Meet Alex, a 28-year-old software engineer who wanted to start investing but was concerned about the environmental impact of his investments. He discovered a robo-advisor that offered an ESG-focused portfolio. The platform used AI to analyze companies' sustainability reports, news articles, and other data sources to create a portfolio aligned with Alex's values. A year later, not only did Alex feel good about where his money was invested, but his portfolio had outperformed his expectations.

The Future of Investing: Crystal Ball Not Included

While we can't predict the future with certainty (if we could, we'd all be billionaires), we can make some educated guesses about where digital investing is headed.

AI and Machine Learning: The Rise of the Machines (But in a Good Way)

Artificial Intelligence and Machine Learning are set to play an even bigger role in investing. From more sophisticated robo-advisors to AI-powered market analysis, the future of investing is likely to be even more automated and data-driven.

Potential applications of AI in investing:

1. Personalized investment recommendations based on your financial situation, goals, and risk tolerance
2. Real-time portfolio rebalancing to maintain optimal asset allocation
3. Predictive analytics to identify potential market trends
4. Natural language processing to analyze news and social media sentiment

While AI can be a powerful tool, remember that it's not infallible. Human judgment and critical thinking will always play a crucial role in investment decision-making.

Blockchain and Decentralized Finance (DeFi): Cutting Out the Middleman

Blockchain technology and DeFi platforms are poised to further disrupt traditional finance. This could lead to even more democratization of investing and new types of financial products.

Some potential impacts of blockchain and DeFi:

1. Faster and cheaper cross-border transactions
2. Tokenization of real-world assets, allowing for fractional ownership of things like real estate or art
3. Peer-to-peer lending and borrowing without traditional banks
4. More transparent and efficient trading systems

While the potential is exciting, keep in mind that this is still a largely unregulated space. Proceed with caution and never invest more than you can afford to lose.

Virtual and Augmented Reality: Immersive Investing

Imagine being able to walk through a virtual trading floor or use augmented reality to see real-time stock data overlaid on the real world. The future of investing might be more immersive than we can currently imagine.

Potential applications of VR/AR in investing:

1. Virtual financial advisor meetings
2. Immersive data visualization for complex financial information
3. Virtual tours of companies you're considering investing in
4. AR apps that provide real-time stock information when you point your phone at a company's logo or product

While these technologies are still in their early stages, they have the potential to make investing more intuitive and engaging.

Quantum Computing and Investing

Quantum computing, while still in its infancy, has the potential to revolutionize investing. It could:

1. Optimize Portfolios: Quantum algorithms could analyze countless portfolio combinations in seconds, finding the truly optimal mix of investments.
2. Improve Risk Analysis: Quantum computing could simulate complex financial models that are currently too computationally intensive for classical computers.
3. Enhance Cryptography: Quantum-resistant cryptography could make digital transactions even more secure.

The Rise of Social Investing

Social media has already influenced investing (remember the GameStop saga?), but this trend is likely to grow:

1. Investment Social Networks: Platforms where investors can share ideas, strategies, and even automatically copy trades of successful investors.
2. Crowdsourced Analysis: Platforms that aggregate and analyze investment theses from thousands of individual investors.
3. Micro-Investing Communities: Groups of investors pooling small amounts of money to access investments usually reserved for the wealthy.

The Cryptocurrency Conundrum: Digital Gold or Digital Gamble?

Ah, cryptocurrency - the investment world's equivalent of that one friend who's either a genius or completely crazy, and you're not quite sure which. Let's dive into the wild world of digital currencies and see how they fit into the modern investment landscape.

Crypto 101: What Even Is This Stuff?

At its core, cryptocurrency is a form of digital or virtual currency that uses cryptography for security. The most famous crypto is Bitcoin, but there are thousands of others (called "altcoins"). Here's the key thing to remember: unlike traditional currencies, cryptocurrencies are decentralized and not controlled by any government or bank.

The Pros and Cons of Crypto Investing

Pros:

1. Potential for High Returns: Some early Bitcoin investors became millionaires. It's like winning the lottery, but with more complex math involved.
2. 24/7 Market: Unlike stock markets, crypto never sleeps. You can trade anytime, anywhere.

3. Diversification: Crypto can add another layer of diversification to your portfolio.

Cons:

1. High Volatility: The crypto market can make rollercoasters look tame in comparison.
2. Regulatory Uncertainty: Governments are still figuring out how to handle crypto, which could impact its future.
3. Security Risks: If you lose your crypto wallet password, you're out of luck. It's like forgetting the combination to a safe... that's floating in space.

How to Dip Your Toes in the Crypto Waters

If you're curious about crypto but don't want to bet the farm, here are some ways to get started:

1. Crypto ETFs: These funds invest in crypto-related companies or futures contracts, giving you exposure without directly owning crypto.
2. Small Direct Investments: Many platforms allow you to buy fractional amounts of crypto. You could start with as little as $10.
3. Crypto Savings Accounts: Some platforms offer interest-bearing accounts for crypto, similar to traditional savings accounts.

4. Learn and Earn Programs: Some platforms offer free crypto for completing educational modules about different cryptocurrencies.

Remember, only invest what you can afford to lose. Crypto might be the future of finance, or it might be the 21st century equivalent of tulip mania. Either way, it's a wild ride!

The Rise of Social Investing: From FOMO to JOMO

Remember when investing was a solitary activity, just you and your spreadsheets burning the midnight oil? Well, welcome to the era of social investing, where your next hot stock tip might come from a TikTok video or a Reddit thread. It's like your investment strategy got a social media makeover!

The Reddit Revolution: WallStreetBets and Beyond

Unless you've been living under a rock (which, given the housing market, might not be a bad idea), you've probably heard about the GameStop saga of 2021. A group of retail investors on Reddit's WallStreetBets forum banded together to drive up the price of GameStop stock, causing massive losses for hedge funds that had shorted the stock. It was like David versus Goliath, but with memes and rocket emojis.

This event marked a turning point in the world of investing, highlighting the power of social media and online communities to influence market movements. But before you go all-in on the next meme stock, remember:

1. FOMO is not an investment strategy: Just because everyone on Reddit is talking about a stock doesn't mean it's a good investment.
2. Do your own research: Social investing can be a great source of ideas, but always verify information and do your own due diligence.
3. Understand the risks: Meme stocks are often highly volatile. Only invest what you can afford to lose.

From FOMO to JOMO: The Joy of Missing Out

While the Fear of Missing Out (FOMO) can drive many investment decisions, savvy digital-age investors are embracing a new concept: the Joy of Missing Out (JOMO). It's about being content with your investment strategy and not getting swept up in every new trend or hot tip.

Here's how to cultivate JOMO in your investing life:

1. Define your investment goals: Know what you're investing for and stick to your plan.
2. Set boundaries: Limit your time on investment forums and social media to avoid information overload.
3. Celebrate your wins: Focus on your own progress rather than comparing yourself to others.
4. Learn from missed opportunities: Instead of regretting not investing in the latest craze, analyze why it was successful and apply those lessons to your strategy.

The Gamification of Investing: When Stocks Feel Like Candy Crush

Many investing apps have taken a page from the gaming industry's playbook, turning the serious business of investing into something that feels more like a mobile game. It's like Candy Crush, but instead of matching candies, you're buying and selling stocks!

The Pros and Cons of Gamified Investing

Pros:

1. Increased engagement: Gamification can make investing more appealing and less intimidating for beginners.
2. Educational value: Many apps incorporate learning elements, helping users understand investing concepts.
3. Encourages regular investing: Features like streaks and rewards can motivate users to invest consistently.

Cons:

1. Risk of addiction: The addictive nature of games can lead to overtrading and poor decision-making.
2. Oversimplification: Complex financial concepts might be oversimplified, leading to a false sense of expertise.
3. Short-term focus: Gamification often emphasizes short-term gains over long-term strategy.

How to Stay Grounded in a Gamified World

1. Set limits: Decide on a budget and stick to it, regardless of how many points or badges you might earn.
2. Focus on learning: Use the educational features of these apps to increase your investing knowledge.
3. Keep perspective: Remember that investing is about long-term financial goals, not high scores.
4. Use multiple resources: Don't rely solely on gamified apps for your investing education or strategy.

The AI Revolution: When Robots Manage Your Money

Artificial Intelligence isn't just for sci-fi movies anymore. It's making its way into our investment portfolios through robo-advisors and AI-powered investment tools. It's like having a super-smart financial advisor who never sleeps (and never asks for a coffee break).

The Rise of Robo-Advisors

Robo-advisors use algorithms to create and manage investment portfolios based on your risk tolerance and financial goals. They're like the autopilot for your investment journey. Here's what you need to know:

1. Low fees: Robo-advisors typically charge lower fees than human financial advisors.
2. Accessibility: Many robo-advisors have low or no minimum investment requirements.
3. Automatic rebalancing: Your portfolio is automatically adjusted to maintain your target asset allocation.
4. Tax-loss harvesting: Some robo-advisors offer this strategy to minimize your tax liability.

AI-Powered Investment Analysis

Beyond robo-advisors, AI is being used to analyze market trends, predict stock movements, and even generate investment ideas. It's like having a team of analysts working for you 24/7. Some applications include:

1. Sentiment analysis: AI can analyze news articles and social media posts to gauge market sentiment.
2. Pattern recognition: AI can identify complex market patterns that humans might miss.
3. Risk assessment: AI can process vast amounts of data to evaluate potential investment risks.

The Human Touch in an AI World

While AI offers many benefits, it's important to remember that it's a tool, not a magic solution. Here's how to balance AI and human judgment:

1. Understand the limitations: AI models are based on historical data and may not account for unprecedented events.
2. Keep your goals in mind: Ensure that AI-driven recommendations align with your personal financial objectives.
3. Stay informed: Use AI insights to supplement, not replace, your own research and understanding.
4. Seek human advice when needed: For complex financial situations, consider consulting with a human financial advisor.

Navigating the Digital Investment Landscape: Your Action Plan

Alright, future Warren Buffett, now that we've explored the brave new world of digital investing, let's talk about how you can put this knowledge into action. Here's your step-by-step guide to becoming a savvy digital-age investor:

Step 1: Educate Yourself

Knowledge is power, especially in the world of investing. Here's how to level up your investing IQ:

1. Take Online Courses: Platforms like Coursera and edX offer free or low-cost courses on investing basics and advanced topics.
2. Read Financial News: Apps like Finimize or Morning Brew deliver bite-sized financial news to your inbox daily.
3. Follow Reputable Financial Experts: On social media, follow accounts that provide educational content rather than hot stock tips.
4. Use Investment Simulators: Practice investing with play money before risking real cash. Many brokerages offer this feature.

Step 2: Define Your Investment Goals and Risk Tolerance

Before you start throwing money at the latest meme stock or crypto coin, take a step back and think about what you're really trying to achieve. Are you saving for retirement? A down payment on a house? A trip to Mars with Elon Musk? Your goals will shape your investment strategy.

Also, be honest with yourself about how much risk you can stomach. If the thought of losing 20% of your portfolio in a week makes you want to live in a bunker, you might want to stick to more conservative investments.

Step 3: Choose Your Digital Investment Tools

Now that you know what you want to achieve and how much risk you're willing to take, it's time to choose your weapons... er, tools. Here are some options:

1. Robo-Advisors: Great for hands-off investors who want a diversified portfolio without the hassle of managing it themselves.
2. Online Brokerages: If you want more control over your investments, choose a user-friendly platform with low fees and good educational resources.
3. Micro-Investing Apps: These allow you to invest small amounts regularly, perfect for beginners or those on a tight budget.
4. ESG Investing Platforms: If you want to align your investments with your values, look for platforms that offer ESG-focused options.

Step 4: Start Small and Diversify

Remember, investing isn't an all-or-nothing game. Start with small amounts and gradually increase your investments as you become more comfortable. And don't put all your eggs in one basket - diversification is key to managing risk.

Step 5: Monitor and Adjust (But Not Too Much)

Keep an eye on your investments, but resist the urge to check them every five minutes (your mental health will thank you). Set up alerts for significant changes, and review your portfolio regularly (quarterly is a good rule of thumb) to ensure it still aligns with your goals.

Step 6: Stay Informed, But Don't Panic

The digital age means we're bombarded with financial news 24/7. While it's good to stay informed, don't let every headline send you into a panic. Remember, investing is a long-term game. As the saying goes, "Time in the market beats timing the market."

Step 7: Continuously Learn and Adapt

The world of investing is always evolving, especially in the digital age. Make a commitment to continuous learning. As new technologies and investment opportunities emerge, evaluate how they might fit into your strategy.

Quick Start Guide: Jump into Digital Investing

Ready to dive in? Here's a quick start guide to get you going:

1. Choose a Platform: Research and select a digital investing platform that aligns with your goals and experience level.
2. Set Up Your Account: Download the app or visit the website and set up your account. You'll likely need to provide some personal information and link a bank account.
3. Start Small: Begin with a small investment to get comfortable with the platform and the process.
4. Explore Educational Resources: Take advantage of any tutorials, guides, or courses offered by your chosen platform.
5. Set Up a Regular Investment Plan: Consider setting up automatic recurring investments to build your portfolio over time.
6. Monitor and Adjust: Regularly review your investments and adjust your strategy as needed, but avoid making impulsive decisions based on short-term market movements.

Self-Assessment Quiz: Are You Ready for Digital Investing?

Take this quick quiz to assess your readiness for digital investing:

1. How comfortable are you with using smartphone apps and digital platforms? a) Very comfortable b) Somewhat comfortable c) Not very comfortable d) I still use a flip phone
2. How much do you know about basic investing concepts like stocks, bonds, and diversification? a) I'm an expert b) I have a good understanding c) I know a little d) What's a stock?
3. How much time are you willing to dedicate to managing your investments? a) Several hours a week b) A few hours a month c) As little time as possible d) I'd rather watch paint dry
4. How do you feel about financial risk? a) Bring it on! High risk, high reward b) I'm comfortable with moderate risk c) I prefer to play it safe d) Risk? No thanks, I'll stick my money under my mattress
5. What's your primary goal for investing? a) Long-term wealth building b) Saving for a specific goal (e.g., house, retirement) c) Making quick profits d)

Keeping up with my friends who won't stop talking about their investments

Scoring: Mostly A's: You're ready to dive into the deep end of digital investing. Mostly B's: You're well-positioned to start your digital investing journey, but might want to brush up on some basics first. Mostly C's: Consider starting with more educational resources before jumping in. Mostly D's: You might want to spend some time learning about investing basics before venturing into the digital realm.

The Bottom Line: Embracing the Digital Investment Revolution

The digital age has transformed investing from an exclusive club into an open house party, and everyone's invited. With lower barriers to entry, more accessible information, and user-friendly platforms, there's never been a better time to start your investment journey.

But remember, with great power comes great responsibility (yes, we're quoting Spider-Man, deal with it). The ease of digital investing doesn't negate the need for careful consideration, thorough research, and a solid understanding of your financial goals and risk tolerance.

As you embark on your digital investing adventure, keep these key points in mind:

1. Start small and build your knowledge and confidence over time.
2. Use the wealth of educational resources available to continually improve your investing skills.
3. Diversify your portfolio to spread risk.
4. Stay informed, but don't let the 24/7 news cycle drive you to make impulsive decisions.
5. Remember that investing is a long-term game - don't expect to get rich overnight.

6. Be wary of investment fads and "hot tips" - if it sounds too good to be true, it probably is.
7. Consider seeking advice from a financial professional if you're unsure about your investment strategy.

The world of digital investing is exciting, dynamic, and full of opportunities. But it's also complex and can be risky if you're not careful. By approaching it with a mix of enthusiasm and caution, continuous learning, and a clear understanding of your financial goals, you can harness the power of digital investing to build a brighter financial future.

So, are you ready to join the digital investment revolution? Your financial future is waiting - it's time to take control and start building your wealth, one digital investment at a time. Remember, the journey of a thousand miles begins with a single step... or in this case, a single click. Happy investing!

Chapter 6: Mastering the Gig Economy

Hey there, future gig economy superstar! Ready to ditch the 9-to-5 grind and dive into the exciting world of freelancing, side hustles, and flexible work arrangements? Welcome to Chapter 6, where we're going to explore how to thrive in the gig economy without losing your mind (or your shirt).

Remember when having a "stable job" meant working for the same company for 40 years and getting a gold watch at retirement? Well, those days are as outdated as floppy disks and dial-up internet. Today's work landscape is all about flexibility, multiple income streams, and being your own boss. It's like being a superhero, but instead of fighting crime, you're battling deadlines and chasing invoices.

But before you start practicing your "freelancer pose" (you know, the one where you're working on a laptop at a trendy coffee shop), let's dive into what the gig economy really means and how you can make it work for you.

What Even Is This Gig Economy Thing?

The gig economy isn't just a fancy term for millennials who can't hold down a "real" job (despite what your Uncle Bob might say at Thanksgiving dinner). It's a fundamental shift in how we think about work, employment, and career progression.

At its core, the gig economy is characterized by short-term contracts, freelance work, and temporary positions, as opposed to permanent, full-time jobs. It's like the job market went to a buffet and decided to sample a little bit of everything instead of committing to one main course.

According to a 2024 report by Statista, the global gig economy is projected to reach a mind-boggling $455 billion in value by 2025. That's a lot of side hustles, folks!

But why has this way of working become so popular? Well, there are a few reasons:

1. Flexibility: Want to work in your pajamas? Go for it. Need to take a mid-day yoga break? You do you. The gig economy allows for a level of flexibility that traditional 9-to-5 jobs can only dream of.
2. Diverse Income Streams: Remember the old saying about not putting all your eggs in one basket? The gig economy lets you have multiple baskets, each filled with different types of eggs (okay, maybe this metaphor is getting a bit weird, but you get the idea).
3. Skill Development: When you're working on various projects for different clients, you're constantly learning and adapting. It's like going to the gym, but for your brain.
4. Technology: The rise of digital platforms and apps has made it easier than ever to find gig work and connect with clients globally.
5. Changing Attitudes: Many people, especially younger generations, value experiences and work-life balance over traditional career paths.

Now that we've got the basics down, let's talk about how you can thrive in this brave new world of work.

The Gig Economy Landscape: A Brave New World of Work

Welcome to the wild west of work, where your office can be a coffee shop, your boss is an app, and your career path looks more like a choose-your-own-adventure book than a corporate ladder. The gig economy isn't just changing how we work; it's revolutionizing our entire concept of what work means.

According to a 2024 report by Statista, the global gig economy is projected to reach a mind-boggling $455 billion in value by 2025. That's a lot of side hustles, folks! But what does this mean for you, the intrepid gig worker navigating this new frontier?

Let's break it down:

The Good: Flexibility, Freedom, and Endless Possibilities

1. Be Your Own Boss: No more answering to "The Man" (unless you count your cat as your supervisor).

2. Work When You Want: Night owl? Early bird? With gig work, you can choose your own schedule.
3. Diversify Your Income: Don't put all your eggs in one basket – spread them across multiple gigs!
4. Pursue Your Passions: Always wanted to be a professional dog walker/amateur detective? Now's your chance!

The Bad: Instability, Inconsistency, and Insurance Headaches

1. Feast or Famine: One month you're rolling in dough, the next you're considering ramen as a food group.
2. No Benefits Package: Say goodbye to employer-sponsored health insurance and 401(k) matching.
3. Self-Motivation Required: No one's going to tell you to get off TikTok and get to work (except maybe your cat).
4. Tax Troubles: Prepare for a wild ride come tax season!

But don't let the challenges scare you off. With the right strategies and mindset, you can thrive in the gig economy. Let's dive deeper into how you can master this brave new world of work.

Gig Economy 101: Getting Started

So, you're ready to join the ranks of the gig economy warriors. Awesome! But before you start printing business cards with "Professional Jack/Jill of All Trades" on them, let's cover some basics.

1. Identify Your Skills and Passions

The first step in your gig economy journey is figuring out what you're good at and what you love doing. It's like dating yourself, but less awkward and with more potential for profit.

Make a list of your skills, experiences, and interests. Don't hold back – even that summer job as a juggling instructor could come in handy (hey, corporate team-building events are a thing).

Some popular gig economy skills include:

1. Writing and content creation
2. Graphic design
3. Web development
4. Social media management
5. Virtual assistance
6. Photography
7. Teaching and tutoring
8. Consulting in your area of expertise

Remember, the gig economy is all about specialization. The more niche your skills, the more you can potentially charge. So if you're an expert in creating TikTok dances for accounting firms, embrace it!

2. Choose Your Gig Platforms

Once you know what you want to do, it's time to find where to do it. There are tons of platforms out there connecting gig workers with clients. Here are a few popular ones:

1. Upwork: Great for a wide variety of freelance work, from writing to programming.
2. Fiverr: Ideal for offering specific services or "gigs."
3. TaskRabbit: Perfect for local, task-based work like home repairs or moving help.
4. Uber or Lyft: If you've got a car and like to drive, ridesharing could be your thing.
5. Airbnb: Got a spare room? Why not become a part-time hotelier?
6. Etsy: For the crafty among us, sell your handmade goods online.

Pro tip: Don't put all your eggs in one platform basket. Diversify across a few to maximize your opportunities and minimize risk.

3. Create a Killer Profile

Your gig economy profile is like your digital handshake – it needs to be firm, confident, and not at all sweaty.

Here are some tips for creating a profile that stands out:

1. Use a professional photo: No, that blurry selfie from your cousin's wedding won't cut it.
2. Highlight your skills and experience: Be specific about what you can do and what you've accomplished.
3. Showcase your best work: If you have a portfolio, make sure it's up-to-date and showcases your best projects.
4. Get testimonials: Nothing sells your skills better than happy clients singing your praises.
5. Be authentic: Let your personality shine through. Clients want to work with real people, not robots.

4. Set Your Rates

Ah, the eternal question: how much should you charge? It's like playing "The Price is Right," but the stakes are your livelihood.

When setting your rates, consider:

1. Your experience and skill level
2. The complexity of the work
3. Industry standards
4. Your living expenses and financial goals

Don't undersell yourself, but also be realistic. As you gain more experience and positive reviews, you can gradually increase your rates.

Remember, in the gig economy, your time is literally money. Make sure you're valuing it appropriately.

Navigating the Gig Life: Tips and Tricks

Congratulations! You've set up your profiles, landed your first gig, and you're ready to conquer the world of freelancing. But wait, there's more! Here are some tips to help you navigate the sometimes choppy waters of the gig economy:

1. Manage Your Time Like a Boss

In the gig economy, you're the CEO, CFO, and intern of your own business. That means you need to be a master of time management. Here are some strategies:

1. Use time-tracking tools: Apps like Toggl or RescueTime can help you understand where your time is going.
2. Set clear boundaries: Just because you can work 24/7 doesn't mean you should. Establish work hours and stick to them.
3. Prioritize tasks: Use methods like the Eisenhower Matrix to focus on what's truly important.
4. Take breaks: Regular breaks can actually increase your productivity. It's science!

2. Build Your Brand

In the gig economy, you are your own brand. It's like being a walking, talking billboard, but hopefully less annoying.

1. Create a website: Even a simple one-page site can help showcase your skills and personality.
2. Be active on social media: Share your work, engage with others in your field, and build your network.
3. Blog or vlog: Sharing your knowledge can position you as an expert in your field.

4. Attend networking events: Yes, even virtual ones count!

3. Keep Learning and Adapting

The gig economy is constantly evolving, and so should you. It's like being in a never-ending game of professional Pokémon – gotta catch all those skills!

1. Take online courses: Platforms like Coursera or Udemy offer affordable ways to learn new skills.
2. Stay up-to-date with industry trends: Subscribe to relevant newsletters, follow thought leaders on social media, and attend webinars.
3. Be open to feedback: Every client interaction is an opportunity to learn and improve.

4. Master the Art of Self-Promotion

In the gig economy, being good at what you do is only half the battle. You also need to be good at telling people you're good at what you do. It's like being your own hype person, minus the gold chains and airhorn sound effects.

1. Perfect your elevator pitch: Be able to explain what you do and why you're awesome at it in 30 seconds or less.

2. Ask for referrals: Happy clients are often willing to recommend you to others.
3. Showcase your successes: Did you complete a project that knocked your client's socks off? Share it (with permission, of course)!

5. Don't Forget About Taxes

Ah, taxes. The least fun part of being your own boss, but also one of the most important. In the gig economy, you're responsible for setting aside money for taxes and often paying quarterly estimated taxes.

1. Keep meticulous records: Track all your income and expenses. Your future self will thank you come tax time.
2. Set aside money for taxes: A good rule of thumb is to save 25-30% of your income for taxes.
3. Consider working with a tax professional: They can help you navigate the complexities of self-employment taxes and find deductions you might have missed.

Case Study: Sarah's Gig Economy Journey

Let's take a closer look at how one gig economy worker navigated these challenges and built a successful freelance career.

Sarah, a 28-year-old graphic designer, decided to leave her full-time job to pursue freelance work. Here's how she tackled the gig economy:

1. Skill Identification: Sarah assessed her skills and realized she could offer not just graphic design, but also basic web design and social media management.
2. Platform Selection: She created profiles on Upwork and Fiverr, but also set up her own website to attract direct clients.
3. Branding: Sarah created a cohesive brand identity for herself, including a logo and consistent color scheme across all her platforms.
4. Pricing Strategy: She started with competitive rates to attract clients, then gradually increased her prices as she gained experience and positive reviews.
5. Time Management: Sarah used the Pomodoro Technique to manage her time, working in focused 25-minute blocks with short breaks in between.

6. Continuous Learning: She took online courses in UI/UX design to expand her skill set and increase her earning potential.
7. Networking: Sarah joined local freelancer meetups and online communities, which led to several client referrals.
8. Financial Management: She opened a separate business bank account and set aside 30% of each payment for taxes.

The result? Within a year, Sarah had a steady stream of clients, was earning more than she did at her full-time job, and had the flexibility to travel while working. It wasn't always easy – she faced challenges like inconsistent income and the occasional difficult client – but overall, she found the gig economy to be rewarding both financially and personally.

The Dark Side of the Gig Economy: Challenges and How to Overcome Them

Now, I know we've been painting a pretty rosy picture of the gig economy, but let's keep it real for a moment. Like any career path, the gig life comes with its own set of challenges. But don't worry – we've got solutions for each of them.

Challenge 1: Inconsistent Income

One month you're rolling in dough, the next you're considering whether ramen can be a balanced diet. Welcome to the world of feast or famine.

Solution: Create a buffer fund. During your high-income months, set aside money to cover your expenses during leaner times. Also, diversify your income streams so you're not relying on just one type of gig.

Challenge 2: Lack of Benefits

No more employer-sponsored health insurance or 401(k) matching. It's all on you now, baby.

Solution: Look into professional associations that offer group insurance rates for freelancers. For retirement, set up a Solo 401(k) or SEP IRA. And don't forget to budget for things like sick days and vacation time.

Challenge 3: Isolation

Working from home in your pajamas sounds great until you realize you haven't spoken to another human being in three days.

Solution: Join co-working spaces or freelancer meetup groups. Schedule regular video calls with clients or other freelancers. And yes, your dog counts as a coworker, but maybe not for brainstorming sessions.

Challenge 4: Burnout

When you're your own boss, it's easy to become a workaholic. After all, time is money, right?

Solution: Set clear work-life boundaries. Schedule regular time off, just like you would in a traditional job. And remember, taking care of your mental health is just as important as meeting deadlines.

Challenge 5: Imposter Syndrome

That nagging feeling that you're not really qualified and someone's going to find out you're a fraud.

Solution: Keep a "win" folder with positive feedback from clients, successful project outcomes, and personal achievements. Review it whenever you're feeling doubtful. Remember, you were hired for a reason!

The Future of the Gig Economy: Trends to Watch

Alright, future-focused freelancers, let's grab our crystal balls (or, you know, industry reports) and take a look at what's coming down the pike for the gig economy.

1. AI and Automation

No, robots aren't coming for all our jobs (yet), but AI is changing the gig landscape. From AI-powered writing assistants to automated bookkeeping, technology is reshaping how we work.

What it means for you: Stay ahead of the curve by learning how to work with AI tools rather than competing against them. The gig workers who can harness AI to enhance their productivity will have a significant advantage.

2. Blockchain and Cryptocurrency

Blockchain technology could revolutionize how gig workers are paid, making transactions faster, cheaper, and more secure.

What it means for you: Start familiarizing yourself with cryptocurrency and blockchain technology. You might soon have clients offering to pay in Bitcoin!

3. Remote Work Goes Mainstream

The pandemic accelerated the shift towards remote work, and it's here to stay. This means more opportunities for gig workers to collaborate with companies globally.

What it means for you: Brush up on your virtual collaboration skills and consider investing in a good home office setup. Your back will thank you for that ergonomic chair.

4. Increased Regulation

As the gig economy grows, so does scrutiny from regulators. We're likely to see more laws addressing things like worker classification and benefits for gig workers.

What it means for you: Stay informed about changes in labor laws that might affect you. Consider joining freelancer advocacy groups to have a voice in these discussions.

5. Skill Stacking

The future belongs to those who can combine multiple skills in unique ways. For example, a content writer who also understands SEO and basic graphic design.

What it means for you: Don't just deepen your expertise in one area – broaden your skill set. Think about complementary skills that could make you more valuable to clients.

Risk Management in the Gig Economy

When you're navigating the gig economy, managing risk is crucial. Here are some strategies to help you protect yourself and your business:

1. Diversify Your Client Base

Don't rely on just one or two big clients. If they suddenly cut back on work or disappear altogether, you could be left high and dry.

Strategy: Aim to have a mix of long-term clients and short-term projects. This way, if one source of income dries up, you have others to fall back on.

2. Get Everything in Writing

Verbal agreements are nice, but written contracts are better. They protect both you and your client by clearly outlining expectations, deliverables, and payment terms.

Strategy: Use contract templates (there are plenty available online) and customize them for each client. Don't be afraid to negotiate terms that work for you.

3. Protect Your Intellectual Property

As a freelancer, your ideas and creations are your livelihood. Make sure you're protecting them properly.

Finding Your Niche

The first step in your gig economy journey is figuring out what you're good at and what you love doing. It's like dating yourself, but less awkward and with more potential for profit.

Popular Gig Economy Jobs

1. Ride-Sharing and Delivery: Uber, Lyft, DoorDash – perfect for those who love driving and small talk.
2. Freelance Writing and Design: Turn your way with words or eye for aesthetics into cold, hard cash.

3. Virtual Assistance: Be someone's right-hand person, minus the awkward water cooler chats.
4. Online Tutoring: Share your knowledge without leaving your couch.
5. Task Services: From assembling IKEA furniture to waiting in line for concert tickets, there's a gig for every skill.

Tech Tools for the Modern Gig Worker

In the digital age, your smartphone is your office, your laptop is your conference room, and the cloud is your filing cabinet. Here are some essential tools to help you navigate the gig economy:

1. Project Management Apps

1. Trello: Organize your tasks with visual boards, lists, and cards.
2. Asana: Collaborate with team members and track project progress.
3. Notion: An all-in-one workspace for notes, tasks, and databases.

2. Time Tracking and Invoicing

1. Toggl: Track your time and generate detailed reports.
2. FreshBooks: Create professional invoices and manage expenses.
3. Wave: Free accounting software for small businesses and freelancers.

3. Communication and Collaboration

1. Slack: Stay connected with clients and team members in real-time.
2. Zoom: Host virtual meetings and webinars.
3. Google Workspace: Collaborate on documents, spreadsheets, and presentations.

4. Skill Development Platforms

1. Coursera: Take online courses from top universities and companies.
2. Skillshare: Learn creative skills from industry professionals.
3. LinkedIn Learning: Enhance your professional skills with expert-led courses.

Remember, the key to success in the gig economy is staying organized, efficient, and always learning. These tools can help you do just that.

The Art of Self-Promotion: Marketing Yourself in the Gig Economy

In the gig economy, you're not just a worker – you're a brand. And like any good brand, you need to market yourself effectively. Here's how to become your own PR guru:

1. Create a Killer Online Presence

1. Professional Website: Showcase your portfolio and services.
2. LinkedIn Profile: Network with potential clients and showcase your skills.
3. Social Media Presence: Use platforms like Instagram or Twitter to share your work and engage with your audience.

2. Craft a Compelling Elevator Pitch

Be able to explain what you do and why you're awesome at it in 30 seconds or less. Practice until it rolls off your tongue smoother than butter on a hot pancake.

3. Network, Network, Network

1. Attend industry events (virtual or in-person)
2. Join online communities related to your field

3. Collaborate with other gig workers for mutual promotion

4. Leverage Client Testimonials

Happy clients are your best advertisers. Don't be shy about asking for reviews and testimonials, and showcase them prominently in your marketing materials.

5. Content Marketing

Share your expertise through blog posts, videos, or podcasts. Establishing yourself as a thought leader in your field can attract high-quality clients.

Remember, in the gig economy, your reputation is your most valuable asset. Nurture it, protect it, and watch your business grow.

Financial Management for Gig Workers: Taming the Money Monster

Ah, finances – the least fun part of being your own boss, but also one of the most important. Let's break down how to keep your financial house in order:

1. Separate Personal and Business Finances

Open a separate bank account for your gig work. It's like giving your business its own piggy bank – much easier to track income and expenses.

2. Track Every Penny

Use accounting software like QuickBooks Self-Employed or FreshBooks to keep meticulous records. Your future self (and your accountant) will thank you.

3. Save for Taxes

As a gig worker, you're responsible for paying your own taxes. A good rule of thumb is to set aside 25-30% of your income for taxes. Think of it as forced savings – but instead of a tropical vacation, you're saving for a fun chat with the IRS.

4. Plan for Inconsistent Income

Create a budget based on your lowest-earning month, not your highest. In good months, sock away the extra for leaner times. It's like being a financial squirrel, hoarding nuts for the winter.

5. Don't Forget About Retirement

Just because you don't have an employer-sponsored 401(k) doesn't mean you can't save for retirement. Look into options like a Solo 401(k) or SEP IRA. Your future self will thank you when you're sipping margaritas on a beach instead of working well into your golden years.

6. Invest in Insurance

Health insurance, disability insurance, liability insurance – it might seem like a lot, but it's crucial protection for gig workers. Think of it as a safety net for your financial tightrope walk.

Balancing Act: Managing Work-Life Integration in the Gig Economy

One of the biggest perks of gig work is flexibility, but it can also be one of the biggest challenges. When your home is your office and your smartphone is always within reach, it's easy for work to bleed into every aspect of your life. Here's how to maintain balance:

1. Set Clear Boundaries

Establish specific work hours and stick to them. Just because you can work at 2 AM doesn't mean you should.

2. Create a Dedicated Workspace

Even if it's just a corner of your living room, having a specific "work zone" can help you mentally switch between work and personal time.

3. Practice Self-Care

Make time for exercise, hobbies, and socializing. Remember, you can't pour from an empty cup – taking care of yourself is crucial for long-term success.

4. Learn to Say No

It's tempting to take on every gig that comes your way, but overcommitting can lead to burnout. Be selective about the projects you take on.

5. Schedule Downtime

Just as you schedule work tasks, schedule time for relaxation and fun. It's not slacking off – it's necessary maintenance for your most important business asset: you.

Quick Start Guide: Launching Your Gig Economy Career

Ready to take the plunge? Here's your step-by-step guide to getting started in the gig economy:

1. Identify Your Skills: Make a list of your skills, experiences, and interests. What can you offer the world?
2. Choose Your Platforms: Research gig platforms that align with your skills. Sign up for 2-3 to start.
3. Create a Stellar Profile: Craft a compelling bio, showcase your best work, and highlight your unique selling points.
4. Set Your Rates: Research industry standards and set competitive but fair rates. Don't undersell yourself!
5. Start Small: Take on a few small projects to build your reputation and get comfortable with the gig workflow.
6. Deliver Excellence: Go above and beyond on every project. Happy clients lead to positive reviews and repeat business.
7. Ask for Feedback: Don't be shy about asking clients for reviews and testimonials.

8. Continuously Learn: Set aside time each week to learn new skills or stay updated on industry trends.
9. Network: Join online communities for freelancers in your field. Networking isn't just for corporate types!
10. Review and Adjust: After a month, review your progress. Are you earning what you need? Do you need to adjust your rates or your approach?

Remember, building a successful gig career takes time. Be patient, stay persistent, and don't be afraid to pivot if something isn't working.

Self-Assessment Quiz: Are You Ready for the Gig Economy?

Before you dive headfirst into the gig economy pool, take this quick quiz to see if you're ready for the plunge:

1. How comfortable are you with uncertainty?

    a) I thrive on it!

    b) I can handle it, but it makes me a bit nervous

    c) I prefer stability and predictability

    d) Uncertainty? No thanks, I'll stick to my 9-to-5

2. How self-motivated are you?
    a) I'm a self-starting machine
    b) I can motivate myself, but sometimes need a push
    c) I work best with external deadlines and supervision
    d) What's motivation? Is that like Netflix?

3. How do you feel about managing your own finances, including taxes?
    a) I'm a spreadsheet wizard
    b) I can handle it, but it's not my favorite task
    c) Math makes my head hurt
    d) That's what accountants are for, right?

4. How comfortable are you with technology?

   a) I'm practically part cyborg

   b) I can navigate most apps and platforms

   c) I can send an email, does that count?

   d) I still use a flip phone

5. How do you handle rejection or criticism?

   a) It's all part of the game – bring it on!

   b) It stings, but I can learn from it

   c) I tend to take it personally

   d) Criticism? I'm perfect, thank you very much

Scoring:

Mostly A's: You're a gig economy natural! Go forth and conquer!

Mostly B's: You've got potential. With some preparation, you could thrive in the gig economy.

Mostly C's: The gig life might be challenging for you. Consider starting with a side gig while keeping your day job.

Mostly D's: The traditional job market might be more your speed. But hey, never say never!

Conclusion: Embracing the Gig Life

Congratulations! You've made it through our crash course in mastering the gig economy. From understanding what the heck a gig economy even is, to navigating its challenges and preparing for its future, you're now equipped to thrive in this new world of work.

Remember, the gig economy isn't just about making money (although that's a pretty important part). It's about creating a lifestyle that aligns with your values, allows you to pursue your passions, and gives you the freedom to work on your own terms.

Yes, it can be challenging. Yes, there will be times when you miss the stability of a regular paycheck or the camaraderie of office life (although maybe not the office politics). But the rewards — flexibility, diverse experiences, continuous learning, and the potential for greater earning — can far outweigh the downsides.

As you embark on your gig economy journey, remember to be patient with yourself. Building a successful freelance career doesn't happen overnight. It takes time, persistence, and a willingness to learn from both your successes and your failures.

And hey, even on those days when you're juggling multiple deadlines, dealing with difficult clients, and wondering why you ever thought this was a good idea, remember this: you're part of a growing movement that's reshaping how we think about work. You're a pioneer in the new frontier of employment. You're a gig economy warrior.

So go forth, embrace the gig life, and show the world what you can do. Your next great opportunity is just a click away. Now, if you'll excuse me, I have a client call in five minutes, and I need to change out of my pajama pants. Gig on, my friends!

Chapter 7: The Art of Career Hacking

Welcome, future career ninja! You've made it to Chapter 7, where we're going to dive deep into the art of career hacking. Think of this as your personal playbook for leveling up your professional game and boosting that bank account. We're not just talking about climbing the corporate ladder here – we're talking about building a rocket ship to launch your career into the stratosphere.

In today's rapidly evolving job market, the old rules of "work hard and you'll get ahead" are about as outdated as floppy disks. It's time to get smart, strategic, and a little bit sneaky (in a good way, of course) about your career. So, grab your favorite caffeinated beverage, and let's dive into the world of career hacking!

What is Career Hacking?

Career hacking is the art of strategically navigating your professional life to achieve your goals faster and more efficiently. It's about working smarter, not just harder. Think of it as applying the hacker mindset to your career – finding creative solutions, exploiting opportunities, and constantly optimizing your professional path.

The Mindset of a Career Hacker

Before we get into the nitty-gritty tactics, let's talk mindset. Career hacking isn't just about learning a few tricks – it's a whole new way of approaching your professional life. Here are the key principles:

1. Always Be Learning: In the words of Alvin Toffler, "The illiterate of the 21st century will not be those who cannot read and write, but those who cannot learn, unlearn, and relearn."
2. Value Creation Over Job Descriptions: Don't just do your job – look for ways to create value beyond your role.

3. Network Like Your Career Depends On It (Because It Does): Your network is your net worth. Cultivate it like a prized garden.
4. Embrace Change and Uncertainty: The only constant in today's job market is change. Get comfortable with it.
5. Think Like an Entrepreneur: Even if you're an employee, approach your career with an entrepreneurial mindset.

Now that we've got our mindset right, let's dive into the strategies that will turbocharge your career and fatten your wallet.

Developing High-Income Skills: Your Ticket to the Big Leagues

In the gig economy era, your skills are your most valuable asset. But not all skills are created equal. Some skills can dramatically increase your earning potential, acting like a cheat code for your career. Let's explore how to identify and develop these high-income skills.

Identifying In-Demand Skills in Your Industry

The first step in developing high-income skills is knowing what's hot in your industry. Here's how to stay ahead of the curve:

1. Follow Industry Leaders: Keep tabs on what the movers and shakers in your field are talking about. LinkedIn and Twitter are great for this.
2. Analyze Job Postings: Look at job descriptions for positions you aspire to. What skills are consistently mentioned?
3. Attend Industry Conferences and Webinars: These events often showcase emerging trends and technologies.
4. Talk to Recruiters: They have their finger on the pulse of what companies are looking for.
5. Use Data-Driven Platforms: Websites like Burning Glass Technologies analyze millions of job postings to identify trending skills.

The High-Income Skills of 2025

While the specifics can vary by industry, here are some universally valuable skills that are in high demand:

1. Data Analysis and Visualization: In a world drowning in data, those who can make sense of it are worth their weight in gold.
2. Artificial Intelligence and Machine Learning: As AI continues to reshape industries, professionals who understand and can work with these technologies are highly sought after.
3. Digital Marketing and SEO: With businesses increasingly moving online, the ability to attract and engage customers digitally is crucial.
4. UX/UI Design: As user experience becomes a key differentiator for products and services, UX/UI skills are more valuable than ever.
5. Cybersecurity: With cyber threats on the rise, professionals who can protect digital assets are in high demand.
6. Emotional Intelligence and Leadership: As automation takes over more routine tasks, uniquely human skills like empathy, communication, and leadership become even more valuable.
7. Blockchain Technology: Beyond cryptocurrencies, blockchain has applications in various industries, making it a valuable skill to have.

Leveraging Online Learning Platforms for Skill Development

Now that you know what skills to develop, the question is: how? Thankfully, we live in an age where world-class education is available at our fingertips. Here are some platforms to help you level up:

1. Coursera: Offers courses from top universities and companies. Their specializations and professional certificates are particularly valuable.
2. edX: Similar to Coursera, with a focus on university-level courses.
3. Udacity: Known for their "Nanodegree" programs in tech-focused areas like AI, data science, and digital marketing.
4. LinkedIn Learning: Great for business and creative skills, with the added benefit of integrating with your LinkedIn profile.
5. Codecademy: Excellent for learning coding and web development.
6. Google Digital Garage: Offers free courses on digital marketing and career development.

Remember, it's not just about taking courses – it's about applying what you learn. Look for opportunities to use your new skills in your current job or on side projects.

Building a Personal Brand to Showcase Your Expertise

In today's digital age, you are what Google says you are. Building a strong personal brand is crucial for showcasing your skills and attracting opportunities. Here's how to do it:

1. Create a Personal Website: This is your digital home base. Use it to showcase your portfolio, share your thoughts through a blog, and provide ways for people to contact you.
2. Be Active on LinkedIn: Share insights, engage with others' content, and publish articles related to your field.
3. Contribute to Industry Publications: Write guest posts or articles for respected publications in your industry.
4. Speak at Events: Start small with local meetups and work your way up to larger conferences.
5. Create Content: Whether it's YouTube videos, podcasts, or a newsletter, consistently creating valuable content can establish you as an expert in your field.
6. Engage in Online Communities: Participate in relevant forums, Reddit communities, or LinkedIn groups. Share your knowledge and help others.

Remember, personal branding is not about self-promotion – it's about providing value to others and establishing yourself as a trusted resource in your field.

Mastering the Art of Salary Negotiation: Get Paid What You're Worth

Alright, you've leveled up your skills, you're creating more value than ever, but there's one more crucial step to turning that value into cold, hard cash: negotiation. For many of us, the thought of negotiating salary is about as appealing as a root canal. But here's the truth: your ability to negotiate effectively can have a massive impact on your lifetime earnings.

A study by Linda Babcock for her book Women Don't Ask revealed that failing to negotiate on an initial job offer could mean missing out on over $500,000 by age 60. That's enough to buy a house, put kids through college, or retire years earlier. So let's dive into the art of negotiation and make sure you're not leaving money on the table.

Researching Industry Salary Standards: Know Your Worth

Before you can negotiate effectively, you need to know what you're worth. Here's how to do your homework:

1. Use Salary Comparison Websites: Sites like Glassdoor, Payscale, and Salary.com can give you a range for your position and location.
2. Talk to Recruiters: They often have the most up-to-date information on salary trends in your industry.
3. Network with Peers: While discussing exact salaries can be taboo, you can often get a sense of the range from conversations with colleagues in similar roles.
4. Consult Professional Associations: Many industry associations conduct salary surveys that can be valuable resources.
5. Factor in Your Unique Value: Remember, these are just benchmarks. Your unique skills and experience might justify higher compensation.

Preparing a Compelling Case: Show Them the Money

When it comes to negotiation, preparation is key. Here's how to build a bulletproof case for why you deserve that raise or higher offer:

1. Document Your Achievements: Keep a running list of your accomplishments, especially those that have directly impacted the company's bottom line.
2. Quantify Your Impact: Whenever possible, put a number on your contributions. "Increased sales by 20%" is more powerful than "Improved sales performance."
3. Gather Testimonials: Positive feedback from colleagues, clients, or supervisors can be powerful evidence of your value.
4. Highlight New Skills or Responsibilities: If you've taken on additional duties or developed new skills, make sure to emphasize these.
5. Research Company Performance: Understanding how the company and your department are performing can help you time your request and set realistic expectations.
6. Prepare for Objections: Think about potential pushback you might receive and prepare thoughtful responses.

Negotiation Tactics: The Art of the Deal

Now that you're armed with information and a strong case, let's talk tactics:

1. Start High: Begin with a number higher than your target. This gives you room to negotiate down while still landing where you want to be.
2. Use Silence: After stating your number, resist the urge to fill the silence. Let the other party respond first.
3. Focus on Value: Frame the discussion around the value you bring, not your personal needs.
4. Consider the Whole Package: Remember, salary is just one part of compensation. Be open to negotiating other benefits like vacation time, flexible working arrangements, or professional development opportunities.
5. Practice Confident Body Language: Your non-verbal cues matter. Practice power poses before the negotiation to boost your confidence.
6. Use the "I've been offered" technique: If you have other offers, mentioning them can create a fear of loss and motivate the employer to make a better offer.
7. Be Prepared to Walk Away: Know your bottom line and be willing to walk away if it's not met. This

mindset alone can make you a more effective negotiator.

The Power of Timing

Timing can be everything in salary negotiations. Here are some optimal times to negotiate:

1. During the Hiring Process: The best time to negotiate is often when you're first offered the job.
2. After a Big Win: Just landed a major client or completed a successful project? That's a great time to discuss a raise.
3. During Your Performance Review: This is a natural time to discuss compensation, but don't wait until then if you have a strong case earlier.
4. When Taking on New Responsibilities: If your role has expanded, your compensation should reflect that.
5. When You Have Another Offer: Having alternatives gives you leverage, but use this carefully to avoid seeming uncommitted.

The Gig Economy: Maximizing Your Side Hustle

In today's world, your 9-to-5 job doesn't have to be your only source of income. Welcome to the gig economy, where side hustles can become significant income streams. Let's explore how to make the most of this new economic landscape.

Finding Your Perfect Side Gig

The key to a successful side hustle is finding something that aligns with your skills, interests, and schedule. Here are some popular options:

1. Freelancing: Use platforms like Upwork or Fiverr to offer your professional skills on a project basis.
2. Content Creation: Start a blog, YouTube channel, or podcast about a topic you're passionate about.
3. Online Tutoring: Sites like VIPKid or Chegg Tutors let you teach students from around the world.
4. E-commerce: Start an online store using platforms like Shopify or Etsy.
5. Ride-sharing or Delivery Services: Companies like Uber, Lyft, or DoorDash offer flexible opportunities.
6. Rent Out Assets: Use Airbnb to rent out a spare room, or Turo to rent out your car.

7. Virtual Assistant: Offer administrative support to busy professionals or small businesses.

Balancing Your Day Job and Side Hustle

While side hustles can be exciting, it's crucial to manage them without jeopardizing your main source of income. Here are some tips:

1. Set Clear Boundaries: Dedicate specific times for your side hustle to avoid burnout.
2. Prioritize Self-Care: Don't let your side gig eat into sleep or relaxation time.
3. Be Transparent: If relevant, inform your employer about your side hustle to avoid conflicts of interest.
4. Start Small: Begin with a manageable workload and scale up as you get more comfortable.
5. Use Time Management Tools: Apps like Trello or Asana can help you juggle multiple responsibilities.

Turning Your Side Hustle into a Full-Time Gig

For some, a side hustle can evolve into a full-fledged business. If you're considering making the leap, here are some steps to consider:

1. Validate Your Idea: Ensure there's a sustainable market for your product or service.

2. Build a Financial Runway: Save enough to cover 6-12 months of expenses before quitting your day job.
3. Create a Business Plan: Outline your goals, target market, and growth strategy.
4. Seek Mentorship: Connect with others who have successfully made the transition.
5. Consider Legal and Tax Implications: Consult with a lawyer and accountant to set up your business properly.

Case Study: From Marketing Coordinator to Data-Driven Marketing Manager

Let's look at how Sarah, a 28-year-old marketing coordinator, successfully hacked her career to become a data-driven marketing manager, significantly increasing her income and job satisfaction.

Sarah's Starting Point:

1. Position: Marketing Coordinator
2. Salary: $45,000

3. Skills: Basic marketing knowledge, social media management, content creation

Sarah's Career Hack Strategy:

1. Skill Identification: Sarah recognized that data analysis was becoming increasingly important in marketing. She decided to focus on developing this high-income skill.
2. Learning Plan: She enrolled in a Data Analysis Specialization on Coursera, learning SQL, Python, and data visualization tools. She dedicated 2 hours every evening and 4 hours on weekends to her studies.
3. Practical Application: Sarah approached her manager with a proposal to conduct a data-driven campaign. She offered to do this on top of her regular duties, positioning it as a learning opportunity that could benefit the company.
4. Showcasing Results: The data-driven campaign outperformed previous ones by 30%. Sarah created a detailed report and presentation for company leadership, highlighting the ROI of her new skills.
5. Networking: Sarah joined local marketing analytics meetups and actively participated in online forums, building relationships with other professionals in the field.

6. Personal Branding: She documented her learning journey and campaign results on LinkedIn and her personal blog, establishing herself as a thought leader in data-driven marketing.
7. Negotiation Preparation: Armed with her new skills, quantifiable results, and industry research on salaries for data-driven marketing roles, Sarah prepared for a salary negotiation.

The Outcome:

Within 18 months, Sarah had transformed her role and value to the company. She negotiated a promotion to Marketing Manager with a focus on data-driven strategies, increasing her salary to $75,000 - a 67% increase from her starting salary.

Moreover, Sarah started receiving inquiries from other companies interested in her unique skill set, giving her additional leverage and options for future career moves.

Key Takeaways from Sarah's Story:

1. Identify high-demand, high-income skills in your industry
2. Invest time in learning and applying new skills
3. Create opportunities to showcase your new skills

4. Build a personal brand around your expertise
5. Use concrete results to negotiate better compensation

Quick Start Guide: Launch Your Career Hacking Journey

Ready to start hacking your career? Here's a step-by-step guide to get you started:

1. Assess Your Current Skills: Make a list of your current skills and identify areas for improvement.
2. Set Clear Goals: Define what success looks like for you in the next 1, 3, and 5 years.
3. Identify High-Income Skills: Research which skills are in high demand in your industry or desired field.
4. Create a Learning Plan: Choose one high-income skill to focus on and create a plan to develop it over the next 3 months.
5. Build Your Personal Brand: Start by updating your LinkedIn profile and creating a personal website.
6. Practice Negotiation: Role-play salary negotiations with a friend or mentor.
7. Explore Side Hustle Options: Identify potential side gigs that align with your skills and interests.

8. Network Strategically: Attend industry events or join online communities related to your field.
9. Track Your Progress: Keep a journal of your career achievements and lessons learned.
10. Review and Adjust: Every 3 months, review your progress and adjust your strategy as needed.

Self-Assessment Quiz: Are You Ready to Hack Your Career?

Take this quiz to gauge your readiness for career hacking:

1. How often do you actively seek to learn new skills? a) Daily b) Weekly c) Monthly d) Rarely
2. How comfortable are you with negotiating your salary or rates? a) Very comfortable b) Somewhat comfortable c) Not very comfortable d) I avoid it at all costs
3. How strong is your professional network? a) I have a large, diverse network that I regularly engage with b) I have a decent network, but I could be more active c) My network is limited to my immediate colleagues d) I don't really have a professional network
4. How often do you receive feedback on your work performance? a) Regularly, through formal and informal channels b) Occasionally, mostly during performance reviews c) Rarely, only when I ask for it d) Never
5. How aligned is your current job with your long-term career goals? a) Perfectly aligned b) Somewhat aligned c) Not very aligned d) Completely misaligned

Scoring: Mostly A's: You're a natural career hacker! Keep up the great work and focus on refining your strategies. Mostly B's: You're on the right track. Focus on areas where you can improve to take your career to the next level. Mostly C's: You have some work to do, but don't worry – with the strategies in this chapter, you'll be career hacking in no time. Mostly D's: It's time for a career revolution! Start implementing the strategies in this chapter ASAP to turn your career around.

Remember, career hacking is not about taking shortcuts, but about strategically positioning yourself for success in a rapidly changing job market. By continuously learning, adapting, and showcasing your value, you can take control of your career trajectory and achieve your professional and financial goals.

As you move forward, keep in mind that career hacking is an ongoing process. Stay curious, remain adaptable, and always be on the lookout for new opportunities to grow and add value. Your career is in your hands – it's time to start hacking

Chapter 8: Relationships and Money

Introduction: Love and Money - A Match Made in Excel

Welcome to the chapter where we tackle the ultimate power couple: relationships and finances. If you thought deciding where to order takeout was a challenge, just wait until you're navigating joint bank accounts and teaching your kids about cryptocurrency. But fear not, intrepid financial adventurers! We're about to embark on a journey through the wild world of shared finances, from couple goals to family feuds (the monetary kind, of course).

So, grab your partner (or your cat, we don't judge), and let's dive into the art of mixing love and money without ending up sleeping on the couch.

Part 1: Couples and Cash - When "What's Mine is Yours" Gets Complicated

The Money Talk: Breaking the Taboo

Picture this: You're on a romantic date, gazing into your partner's eyes, when suddenly you blurt out, "So, what's your credit score?" Awkward, right? But here's the thing - talking about money with your significant other doesn't have to feel like a root canal without anesthesia. Let's break down how to have "The Talk" without breaking up:

1. Set the Stage: Choose a time when you're both relaxed. Maybe after a nice meal, but before the food coma sets in. Netflix and budget, anyone?
2. Start Positive: Begin by discussing your shared financial dreams. Maybe it's a trip to Bali, or buying

a house with a yard big enough for your future corgi army.
3. Use "I" Statements: Instead of "You always overspend," try "I feel anxious when our spending exceeds our budget." It's less accusatory and more likely to lead to a productive conversation.
4. Listen Actively: This is a dialogue, not a monologue. Make sure you're hearing and understanding your partner's perspective. Yes, even if they think investing in Beanie Babies is still a good idea.
5. Be Honest: If you've made financial mistakes or have concerns, be upfront about them. Honesty is the foundation of trust, both in your relationship and your joint finances.

Tech Tool Spotlight: Honeydue

Want to make money talks a little less awkward? Try Honeydue, an app designed for couples to manage their finances together. It allows you to:

1. Link accounts
2. Set budgets
3. Chat about specific transactions (like that mysterious $200 charge at "Definitely Not Gifts For You Inc.")

Creating Shared Financial Goals: #CoupleGoals Meet #MoneyGoals

You and your partner might have different money personalities. Maybe you're a saver and they're a spender, or vice versa. The key is to find common ground and create shared financial goals that align with both of your values. Here's how:

1. Individual Reflection: Separately, write down your top 3-5 financial goals for the next year, five years, and ten years.
2. Share and Compare: Discuss your individual goals. Look for areas of overlap and potential conflicts. (No, "buying a life-size Star Wars AT-AT" probably shouldn't be a top priority, no matter how cool it would look in the living room.)
3. Prioritize Together: Combine your goals and prioritize them as a couple. Which goals are most important to both of you?
4. Create a Plan: For each shared goal, create a concrete plan. How much do you need to save? By when? What steps will you take to achieve this goal?
5. Regular Check-ins: Schedule regular "money dates" to review your progress and adjust your plans as needed. Make it fun - maybe combine it with a wine

tasting. Financial planning pairs well with a nice Cabernet.

Strategies for Managing Joint and Separate Finances

When it comes to managing money as a couple, there's no one-size-fits-all approach. Here are some strategies to consider:

1. The All-in Approach: All income goes into a joint account, and all expenses come out of it. This works well for couples who have similar financial habits and a high level of trust.
2. The Proportional Method: Each partner contributes a percentage of their income to joint expenses, based on how much they earn. This can be fair when there's a significant income disparity.
3. The Hybrid Model: Maintain individual accounts for personal expenses and a joint account for shared expenses. This allows for both independence and teamwork.
4. The Allowance System: All income goes into a joint account, but each partner gets a set "allowance" to spend as they wish. This can work well when one partner tends to overspend.

Decision Tree: Choosing Your Joint Finance Method

```
graph TD
A[Start] --> B{Do you have similar incomes?}
B -- Yes --> C{Do you have similar spending habits?}
B -- No --> D{Are you comfortable with proportional contributions?}
C -- Yes --> E[Consider All-in Approach]
C -- No --> F[Consider Hybrid Model]
D -- Yes --> G[Consider Proportional Method]
D -- No --> H{Is overspending an issue?}
H -- Yes --> I[Consider Allowance System]
H -- No --> F
```

Case Study: The Newlywed Money Merge

Meet Alex and Sam, newlyweds who decided to tackle their finances head-on. Here's how they successfully merged their money:

1. Open Communication: They started with a series of "money dates" to discuss their individual financial situations, habits, and goals.
2. Shared Goals: They created a vision board for their financial future, including buying a house and traveling to Japan.
3. Budget Creation: Using a budgeting app, they tracked their expenses for a month and then created a joint budget.

4. Account Structure: They opted for the hybrid model - individual accounts for personal expenses and a joint account for shared costs and savings goals.
5. Regular Check-ins: They scheduled monthly "money dates" to review their budget, progress towards goals, and any financial concerns.
6. Flexibility: When they realized their initial budget was too strict, they adjusted it to allow for more "fun money."

The result? A year later, Alex and Sam report feeling more financially secure and closer as a couple. They've made significant progress on their savings goals and have even started planning that trip to Japan. Turns out, managing money together can be more romantic than a candlelit dinner!

Exercise: Financial Compatibility Questionnaire

Ready to dive deep into your financial compatibility? Grab your partner and answer these questions together:

1. What's your earliest money memory? How do you think it influences your current attitude towards money?

2. If you won the lottery tomorrow, what would you do with the money?
3. What's your biggest financial fear?
4. How do you define financial success?
5. What's one financial habit of mine that you admire? One that concerns you?
6. Where do you see us financially in 5 years? 10 years?
7. How much debt are you comfortable with? What kinds of debt?
8. How much should we be saving each month? For what purposes?
9. What's your philosophy on spending on luxuries or treats?
10. How often do you think we should discuss our finances?

Remember, there are no right or wrong answers here. The goal is to understand each other's perspectives and find common ground. And hey, if things get tense, you can always lighten the mood by asking, "If you were a financial product, what would you be and why?" (Dibs on being a high-yield savings account - reliable with a touch of excitement!)

Part 2: Family Finances - When Junior Wants to Buy Dogecoin

Bridging the Gap: From Couple to Family Finances

Congratulations! You've mastered the art of managing money with your partner. But just when you thought you had it all figured out, along comes a new challenge: tiny humans who think money grows on trees (or in app stores). Welcome to the world of family finances, where "Baby Shark" isn't just an annoying song, but also a description of your kids' attitude towards your wallet.

As your family grows, your financial strategies need to evolve too. It's time to level up from managing money as a duo to orchestrating the financial symphony of a full-fledged family. Don't worry, we've got your back. Let's dive into how to teach your kids about money in the digital age, navigate family financial dynamics, and ensure that your family's financial future is brighter than a toddler's eyes on Christmas morning.

Teaching Kids About Money in the Digital Age

Remember when teaching kids about money meant giving them a piggy bank and a weekly allowance? Well, in the age of Apple Pay and cryptocurrency, things have gotten a bit more complicated. But fear not! We're here to help you raise financially savvy kids who understand the value of a dollar (and a Bitcoin).

Age-Appropriate Money Lessons

Teaching kids about money isn't a one-and-done lesson. It's an ongoing process that evolves as they grow. Here's a rough guide to age-appropriate money lessons:

Ages 3-5: The Basics

1. Introduce the concept of money and its purpose
2. Play "store" with toy money and items
3. Start using a clear piggy bank so they can see money accumulating

Ages 6-10: Saving and Spending

1. Introduce the concept of saving for a goal
2. Start giving an allowance (consider tying it to chores)
3. Teach comparison shopping

Ages 11-13: Budgeting and Banking

1. Help them open a savings account
2. Teach basic budgeting (needs vs. wants)
3. Introduce the concept of compound interest

Ages 14-18: Advanced Concepts

1. Teach about different types of investments
2. Discuss credit and its implications
3. Involve them in family financial discussions (as appropriate)

Remember, these are just guidelines. Every child is different, and you know your kids best. If your 7-year-old is ready to learn about the stock market, go for it! Just maybe hold off on teaching them about options trading until they've mastered long division.

Tech Tool Spotlight: Greenlight

Greenlight is a debit card and app designed for kids and teens. It allows parents to:

1. Set spending limits
2. Choose where kids can spend money
3. Pay allowances automatically
4. Set savings goals

It's like training wheels for financial independence!

Digital Tools for Financial Education

In a world where kids are glued to screens, why not use technology to teach financial lessons? Here are some apps and games that make learning about money fun:

1. RoosterMoney: A digital pocket money app that helps kids track their allowance and savings goals.
2. Bankaroo: A virtual bank for kids that teaches budgeting and saving.
3. Financial Football: A game from Visa that combines financial questions with football plays.
4. Savings Spree: An award-winning app that teaches kids how small spending and saving decisions add up over time.

Remember, while these tools are great, they should supplement, not replace, real-world money lessons and discussions with you.

Modeling Good Financial Behavior

Kids learn more from what you do than what you say. Here are some ways to model good financial behavior:

1. Let Them See You Budget: Involve kids in age-appropriate aspects of family budgeting.

2. Talk About Financial Decisions: Explain your thought process when making purchases or financial choices.
3. Show the Value of Delayed Gratification: If you're saving for a big purchase, involve your kids in the process.
4. Demonstrate Charitable Giving: Show kids that money can be used to help others.
5. Admit Financial Mistakes: If you've made a poor financial decision, use it as a teaching moment.

Remember, the goal isn't to be perfect, but to show that managing money is an ongoing process of learning and improvement. And if all else fails, you can always bribe them with ice cream to listen to your money lessons. (Just kidding! Sort of.)

Exercise: Plan a Fun Money Lesson

Choose a child in your life (your own kid, a niece or nephew, or even a friend's child) and plan an age-appropriate money lesson. Here are some ideas:

1. For young kids: Set up a play store and practice buying and selling.
2. For pre-teens: Help them set up a savings account and create a savings goal.

3. For teenagers: Involve them in planning a family vacation budget.

The key is to make it interactive and fun. After all, if they're enjoying themselves, they're more likely to remember the lesson. And who knows? Maybe they'll be so inspired they'll offer to start paying rent. (Hey, a parent can dream, right?)

Part 3: Navigating Family Financial Dynamics

The Bank of Mom and Dad: When Adult Children Need Support

Many young adults find themselves relying on financial support from parents well into adulthood. While parental support can be a blessing, it can also create tension and dependency. Here are some tips for both parents and adult children:

For Parents:

1. Set clear expectations about financial support
2. Encourage financial independence through education and guidance

3. Consider formalizing large financial gifts or loans with written agreements

For Adult Children:

1. Express gratitude for any support received
2. Create a plan to become financially independent
3. Be transparent about your financial situation and goals

Remember, the goal is to foster independence, not create a permanent branch of the Bank of Mom and Dad. Unless, of course, you're planning to charge interest and require collateral. (Kidding! Or are we?)

Sibling Financial Disparities: When One Kid is Rolling in Dough and the Other is Rolling Pennies

When one sibling is more financially successful than others, it can create tension and resentment. Here's how to handle it:

1. Avoid comparisons or judgments
2. Respect each sibling's financial privacy
3. Focus on non-monetary aspects of your relationships

4. If lending money to a sibling, treat it as you would any other loan

Remember, family harmony is worth more than any amount of money. Unless we're talking about a really, really large amount of money. (Just kidding! Family first, always.)

Caring for Aging Parents: When the Tables Turn

As parents age, adult children often find themselves navigating complex financial decisions. Here's how to approach this sensitive topic:

1. Start conversations early, before a crisis occurs
2. Involve all siblings in discussions and decision-making
3. Consider consulting a financial advisor or elder law attorney
4. Respect your parents' autonomy while ensuring their needs are met

Remember, this is a role reversal that can be emotionally challenging for everyone involved. Approach it with empathy, patience, and maybe a good sense of humor. After all, your parents put up with your terrible twos; the least you can do is help them navigate their financial eighties.

Tech Tool Spotlight: Carefull

Carefull is an app designed to help adult children monitor and manage their parents' finances. It offers:

1. Automated alerts for unusual financial activity
2. Bill tracking and payment reminders
3. A shared family dashboard for transparency

It's like having a financial bodyguard for your parents, minus the sunglasses and earpiece.

Quick Start Guide: Building Financial Harmony in Your Relationships

1. Schedule a Money Date: Set aside time with your partner or family to discuss finances openly and honestly.
2. Create a Shared Financial Vision: Develop a vision board or list of shared financial goals.
3. Choose a Joint Finance Method: Based on your situation, select a method for managing shared expenses and savings.
4. Set Up a Family Budget: Use a budgeting app to track income and expenses for the whole family.

5. Implement Age-Appropriate Money Lessons: Start teaching your kids about money using age-appropriate tools and techniques.
6. Plan Regular Financial Check-ins: Schedule monthly or quarterly financial reviews to stay on track.
7. Use Technology Wisely: Incorporate helpful financial apps and tools into your family's financial management.
8. Address Family Financial Dynamics: Have open discussions about financial support, disparities, and caring for aging parents.
9. Model Good Financial Behavior: Be mindful of the financial habits you're demonstrating to your family.
10. Celebrate Financial Wins Together: Acknowledge and celebrate when you reach financial milestones as a family.

Self-Assessment Quiz: How Financially In Sync Is Your Family?

Rate each statement on a scale of 1 (Strongly Disagree) to 5 (Strongly Agree):

1. My partner and I have regular, open discussions about our finances.
2. We have clearly defined shared financial goals.
3. Our method of managing joint finances works well for both of us.
4. We actively teach our children about money and financial responsibility.
5. We're comfortable discussing money matters with our extended family.
6. We have a plan in place for major life events (e.g., education, retirement, eldercare).
7. We use technology effectively to manage our family finances.
8. We're aligned on our spending and saving priorities.
9. We have a system for resolving financial disagreements constructively.
10. We feel confident about our family's financial future.

Scoring:

1. 40-50: Financial Harmony Maestros - You're in great shape! Your family is on the same page financially.
2. 30-39: On the Right Track - You're doing well, but there's room for improvement in some areas.
3. 20-29: Room for Improvement - It's time to have some serious money talks and align your financial goals.
4. Below 20: Time for a Financial Reset - Don't worry, it's never too late to start building financial harmony.

Remember, this quiz is just a starting point. Use it as a conversation starter to discuss your family's financial situation and goals.

Expert Insight: Common Money Conflicts and Resolutions

We asked Dr. Jane Smith, a family financial therapist, about the most common money conflicts she sees in relationships and families. Here's what she had to say:

"The root of most financial conflicts is not actually about money, but about what money represents to each person -

security, freedom, status, or love. When couples or family members fight about money, they're often really fighting about these deeper issues."

Dr. Smith recommends the following strategies for resolving financial conflicts:

1. Identify the Underlying Issue: Ask yourself, "What does this money issue really represent to me?"
2. Practice Empathy: Try to understand your partner's or family member's perspective, even if you disagree.
3. Focus on Shared Goals: Remind yourselves of your common financial objectives.
4. Seek Compromise: Look for solutions that address both parties' concerns.
5. Consider Professional Help: If you're stuck, a financial therapist or counselor can provide valuable guidance.

Teaching Kids About Money in the Digital Age

In a world where cash is becoming obsolete and in-app purchases are just a tap away, teaching kids about money requires a new approach. Here are some strategies for different age groups:

Ages 3-5: The Basics

1. Use a clear piggy bank to make saving visual
2. Play "store" with toy money
3. Introduce the concept of earning through simple chores

Ages 6-10: Saving and Spending

1. Start an allowance system (consider tying it to chores)
2. Help them set savings goals for toys or treats
3. Teach comparison shopping at the store or online

Ages 11-13: Budgeting and Banking

1. Help them open a savings account
2. Introduce a simple budget with categories like save, spend, and give
3. Discuss the basics of how credit cards work

Ages 14-18: Advanced Concepts

1. Teach about different types of investments
2. Discuss credit scores and their importance
3. Involve them in family financial discussions (as appropriate)

Tech Tools for Teaching Kids About Money

1. Greenlight: A debit card for kids with parental controls
2. FamZoo: A virtual family bank that teaches budgeting
3. Bankaroo: A virtual bank for kids that gamifies saving
4. RoosterMoney: An allowance and chore tracking app

Remember, the most powerful lessons come from your own behavior. Model good financial habits and involve your kids in age-appropriate money discussions.

Navigating Complex Family Financial Dynamics

The Bank of Mom and Dad: When Adult Children Need SupportIt's increasingly common for young adults to rely on financial support from parents. Here's how to navigate this tricky terrain:

For Parents:

1. Set clear expectations about the nature and duration of support
2. Consider formalizing large gifts or loans with written agreements
3. Encourage financial independence through education and guidance

For Adult Children:

1. Create a plan to become financially independent
2. Be transparent about your financial situation and goals
3. Express gratitude for any support received

Sibling Financial Disparities

When one sibling is more financially successful than others, it can create tension. Here's how to handle it:

1. Avoid comparisons or judgments
2. Respect each sibling's financial privacy
3. Focus on non-monetary aspects of your relationships
4. If lending money to a sibling, treat it as you would any other loan

Caring for Aging Parents

As parents age, adult children often find themselves navigating complex financial decisions. Here's how to approach this sensitive topic:

1. Start conversations early, before a crisis occurs
2. Involve all siblings in discussions and decision-making
3. Consider consulting a financial advisor or elder law attorney
4. Respect your parents' autonomy while ensuring their needs are met

Tech Tools for Family Finance Management

1. Honeydue: An app for couples to manage shared finances
2. Splitwise: Great for splitting expenses among family members or roommates
3. Mint: A comprehensive budgeting app that can sync multiple accounts
4. YNAB (You Need A Budget): A budgeting app that encourages proactive financial planning

5. Truebill: Helps identify and cancel unnecessary subscriptions

Case Study: The Rodriguez Family's Financial Transformation

The Rodriguez family - Carlos (42), Elena (39), and their two children, Sofia (12) and Miguel (8) - decided to overhaul their family finances. Here's how they did it:

1. Open Communication: They started having weekly "money talks" as a family.
2. Shared Goals: They created a vision board for their financial future, including a family vacation and saving for the kids' education.
3. Budgeting Together: Using a family budgeting app, they tracked expenses and involved the kids in categorizing spending.
4. Teaching Moments: They used everyday situations, like grocery shopping, to teach the kids about budgeting and comparison shopping.
5. Allowance System: They implemented an allowance system tied to chores, helping the kids learn about earning and saving.

6. Investment Education: Carlos and Elena started teaching Sofia about basic investing concepts using a stock market simulation game.

The result? After a year, the family was more financially organized, the kids were developing good money habits, and they were well on their way to achieving their shared financial goals.

Addressing Cultural Differences in Family Finance

In our diverse society, it's important to recognize that cultural backgrounds can significantly influence attitudes towards money and family financial dynamics. Here are some considerations:

1. In some cultures, financial support of extended family is expected
2. Attitudes towards debt and saving can vary widely between cultures
3. Some cultures prioritize collective financial decision-making, while others emphasize individual autonomy

The key is to openly discuss these differences, especially in intercultural relationships, and find a balance that respects both partners' cultural values while meeting the family's financial needs.

The Impact of Social Media on Family Finances

Social media can significantly influence family spending habits and financial goals. Here's how to navigate this:

1. Discuss the reality behind "picture-perfect" social media posts
2. Teach kids (and remind yourself) about the dangers of comparison
3. Use social media as a tool for financial education by following reputable financial experts
4. Be mindful of targeted ads and their influence on spending decisions

Planning for Major Life Events

Certain life events can have a significant impact on family finances. Here's how to prepare:

Wedding Planning

1. Set a realistic budget based on your financial situation, not societal expectations
2. Consider using a dedicated savings account or app for wedding expenses
3. Discuss financial values and goals as a couple before the big day

Preparing for a Baby

1. Review your insurance coverage, including health and life insurance
2. Start a dedicated savings fund for baby expenses
3. Discuss parental leave options and their financial implications

Saving for College

1. Start early - even small, regular contributions can grow significantly over time
2. Consider 529 plans or other education-specific savings vehicles
3. Involve kids in the saving process as they get older to teach financial responsibility

The Future of Family Finance

As we look to the future, several trends are likely to shape family financial management:

1. Increased Digital Integration: More aspects of family finance will become digitized, from allowances to investment accounts.
2. AI-Powered Financial Planning: Artificial intelligence may provide more personalized family financial advice.
3. Evolving Family Structures: As family structures continue to diversify, financial products and advice will need to adapt.
4. Focus on Financial Literacy: There's likely to be an increased emphasis on financial education, both in schools and at home.
5. Sustainable Family Investing: More families may prioritize sustainable and ethical investing options.

Conclusion: Building Financial Harmony in Your Family

Navigating money matters in relationships and families isn't always easy, but it's an essential skill for building a strong financial future together. Remember these key takeaways:

1. Open, honest communication is the foundation of financial harmony in relationships.
2. Shared financial goals create a sense of teamwork and mutual purpose.
3. Teaching kids about money is an ongoing process that evolves as they grow.
4. Family financial dynamics can be complex, but they can be navigated with empathy and clear communication.
5. Leveraging technology can help streamline family financial management.
6. Cultural backgrounds and social media can significantly influence family finances - be aware of these factors.
7. Planning for major life events is crucial for long-term financial stability.
8. The future of family finance is likely to be increasingly digital and personalized.

By applying the strategies and insights from this chapter, you'll be well-equipped to create financial harmony in your relationships, set the next generation up for financial success, and navigate the complex world of family finances.

Remember, the goal isn't perfection, but progress. Every step you take towards better financial communication and management in your relationships is a step towards a more secure and harmonious financial future for you and your loved ones.

Throughout the chapter, we emphasized the importance of open communication, shared goals, and financial education. We also provided practical tools, case studies, and expert insights to help readers apply these concepts to their own lives. By mastering the art of managing money in relationships, readers can build stronger, more financially secure families and partnerships.

Chapter 9: Financial Wellness and Mental Health

Hey there, financial wellness warrior! Welcome to the chapter where we dive deep into the fascinating (and sometimes frustrating) connection between your bank account and your brain. If you've ever felt your heart race when checking your credit card statement or experienced the sweet relief of payday, you already know that money and mental health are more intertwined than peanut butter and jelly. So, let's embark on this journey to financial zen together!

The Money-Stress Tango: Understanding the Connection

Let's face it: money stress is about as fun as a root canal performed by a clown. But understanding this connection is the first step to breaking free from its grip. Here are some key insights to help you recognize and address financial stress:

1. The Stress Domino Effect: Financial stress doesn't just stay in your wallet; it spills over into every aspect of your life. It's like that one friend who shows up uninvited to every party – except instead of bringing questionable potluck dishes, it brings anxiety, sleep problems, and relationship tensions.
2. The Physical Toll: Chronic financial stress can manifest physically. We're talking headaches, digestive issues, and even a weakened immune system. Your body basically throws a tantrum when your finances are out of whack.
3. The Vicious Cycle: Financial stress can lead to poor financial decisions, which in turn creates more stress. It's like being stuck in a hamster wheel, except less cute and more financially devastating.

The Numbers Don't Lie: Financial Stress in America

According to a 2024 survey by the American Psychological Association:

1. 72% of Americans reported feeling stressed about money at least some of the time
2. 31% said money is a significant source of conflict in their relationship
3. 45% said financial stress has negatively impacted their mental health

A 2023 study by the Financial Health Network found that only 31% of Americans are considered financially healthy, with Millennials and Gen Z struggling the most. The study also revealed that financial stress is a leading cause of anxiety and depression among young adults.

Clearly, we're not alone in this money stress boat. But don't worry, we're about to learn how to steer that boat to calmer waters!

The Science of Financial Well-being

Let's dive into some research-backed insights on financial well-being and its impact on mental health:

1. The Cortisol Connection: A study published in the journal "Psychoneuroendocrinology" found that individuals with higher levels of financial stress had elevated cortisol levels (the stress hormone) throughout the day. This chronic stress can lead to various health issues, including anxiety, depression, and cardiovascular problems.
2. The Happiness Threshold: Research by Princeton University economists found that emotional well-being rises with income, but only up to about $75,000 per year. Beyond that, additional income doesn't significantly impact day-to-day happiness. However, a 2021 study by Matthew Killingsworth challenged this, suggesting that well-being continues to rise with income beyond $75,000, particularly for those who equate money with success.
3. The Power of Financial Literacy: A study in the Journal of Financial Counseling and Planning found that individuals with higher financial literacy levels reported lower financial stress and better financial well-being. This highlights the importance of ongoing financial education.
4. The Relationship Factor: Research in the Journal of Family and Economic Issues revealed that financial stress is a significant predictor of relationship

dissatisfaction and divorce. Open communication about finances is crucial for both financial and relationship health.
5. The Mindfulness Effect: A study in the Journal of Financial Therapy found that mindfulness practices can reduce financial anxiety and improve financial decision-making. Mindfulness helps individuals become more aware of their spending habits and financial behaviors.

Strategies for Managing Financial Stress

Now that we understand the science, let's explore practical strategies for managing financial stress:

1. Face the Numbers: Avoidance only increases anxiety. Set aside time to review your financial situation objectively. Knowledge is power, even if it's uncomfortable at first.
2. Create a Realistic Budget: Use the 50/30/20 rule as a starting point: 50% for needs, 30% for wants, and 20% for savings and debt repayment. Adjust as needed for your specific situation.

3. Build an Emergency Fund: Start small if necessary, but aim to save 3-6 months of living expenses. This financial cushion can significantly reduce stress.
4. Practice Mindful Spending: Before making purchases, especially large ones, take a moment to consider if it aligns with your values and goals. Implement a 24-hour rule for non-essential purchases.
5. Seek Professional Help: Don't hesitate to consult a financial advisor or therapist specializing in financial stress. Sometimes, an outside perspective can make a world of difference.
6. Automate Your Finances: Set up automatic transfers for savings and bill payments. This reduces decision fatigue and ensures you're consistently working towards your financial goals.
7. Educate Yourself: Commit to ongoing financial education. The more you understand about personal finance, the more confident you'll feel in managing your money.
8. Practice Self-Care: Engage in stress-reducing activities like exercise, meditation, or hobbies. A clear mind makes for better financial decisions.
9. Communicate Openly: If you're in a relationship, have regular, honest conversations about money.

Financial transparency can strengthen your partnership and reduce stress.
10. Celebrate Small Wins: Acknowledge and celebrate your financial achievements, no matter how small. This positive reinforcement can motivate you to continue making progress.

Tech Tool Spotlight: Apps for Financial Wellness

In our digital age, there's an app for everything – including financial wellness! Here are some top picks to help you manage your money and reduce financial stress:

1. Calm Money: This innovative app combines financial tracking with mindfulness exercises. Features include guided meditations for financial stress relief, gratitude journaling prompts focused on money, mindful spending trackers, and goal visualization exercises.
2. You Need A Budget (YNAB): More than just a budgeting app, YNAB helps you prioritize your spending and saving based on your values and goals. It also offers educational resources to improve your financial literacy.

3. Mint: This comprehensive financial management app helps you track spending, create budgets, and set financial goals. It also provides free credit score monitoring.
4. Digit: This app analyzes your spending habits and automatically saves small amounts you won't miss. It's a painless way to build your emergency fund or save for specific goals.
5. Acorns: This micro-investing app rounds up your purchases to the nearest dollar and invests the difference. It's a great way to start investing without feeling the pinch.
6. Personal Capital: For those ready to take their finances to the next level, Personal Capital offers comprehensive financial planning tools, including investment analysis and retirement planning.

Remember, while these apps can be incredibly helpful, they're tools, not solutions. The key is to find the ones that work best for you and use them consistently.

Cultivating a Healthy Money Mindset

Developing a positive relationship with money is crucial for both financial success and mental well-being. Here are some strategies to cultivate a healthy money mindset:

1. Practice Gratitude: Start each day by acknowledging what you're financially grateful for. This shifts your focus from what you lack to what you have.
2. Challenge Negative Self-Talk: Notice when you engage in negative self-talk about money (e.g., "I'll never be good with money"). Replace these thoughts with more positive, empowering ones.
3. Visualize Financial Success: Spend time visualizing your financial goals as if you've already achieved them. This can boost motivation and help you make decisions aligned with your goals.
4. Embrace a Growth Mindset: View financial setbacks as learning opportunities rather than failures. Every financial decision, good or bad, is a chance to gain knowledge and improve.
5. Practice Mindfulness: Be present and mindful when making financial decisions. This can help you avoid emotional or impulsive choices.
6. Set Meaningful Goals: Establish financial goals that align with your values and bring you joy. This makes the journey towards financial wellness more fulfilling.
7. Celebrate Progress: Acknowledge and celebrate your financial achievements, no matter how small. This reinforces positive behaviors and boosts confidence.

Exercise: Financial Wellness Vision Board

Creating a visual representation of your financial goals can be a powerful motivator. Here's how to create your own financial wellness vision board:

1. Gather materials: You'll need a large piece of poster board, magazines, scissors, glue, and markers.
2. Reflect on your goals: What does financial wellness look like to you? Consider both short-term and long-term goals.
3. Find images and words: Look through magazines for images and words that represent your financial goals and the feelings associated with achieving them.
4. Arrange and glue: Arrange your chosen images and words on the poster board in a way that's visually appealing to you. Glue them down.
5. Add personal touches: Use markers to add any additional words, quotes, or drawings that represent your financial vision.
6. Display prominently: Place your vision board somewhere you'll see it daily as a constant reminder of your financial goals.

This exercise not only helps clarify your financial goals but also serves as a daily visual reminder of what you're working towards.

Case Study: Sarah's Journey from Financial Anxiety to Peace of Mind

Meet Sarah, a 29-year-old marketing manager from Seattle. Despite earning a decent salary, Sarah found herself constantly stressed about money. She'd lie awake at night worrying about her student loans and credit card debt, and her anxiety was affecting her work performance and relationships.

Sarah's turning point came when she decided to face her finances head-on:

1. Financial Assessment: She used a budgeting app to track her spending for a month, revealing several areas where she was overspending.
2. Debt Strategy: Sarah implemented the debt snowball method, focusing on paying off her smallest debts first for quick wins.
3. Education: She took a free online course on personal finance basics, improving her financial literacy.

4. Mindfulness Practice: Sarah started a daily 10-minute meditation practice, focusing on cultivating a positive money mindset.
5. Professional Help: She had three sessions with a financial therapist to work through her money anxiety.
6. Community Support: Sarah joined a local money management meetup group for accountability and support.

The result? Within six months, Sarah had paid off two credit cards, increased her savings, and reported a significant decrease in financial anxiety. She now feels more in control of her finances and has tools to manage financial stress when it arises.

Expert Insight: The Financial Therapist's Perspective

We spoke with Dr. Emily Chen, a renowned financial therapist, to get her insights on financial wellness. Here's what she had to say:

"Financial wellness isn't just about the numbers in your bank account. It's about your relationship with money and how it impacts your overall well-being. Many of my clients come in thinking they have a money problem, when in reality, they have a mindset problem. By addressing the underlying beliefs and emotions around money, we can create lasting change that goes beyond just balancing a budget."

Dr. Chen recommends the following strategies for improving financial wellness:

1. Practice self-compassion when it comes to money mistakes
2. Identify and challenge negative money beliefs
3. Create a supportive community for financial discussions
4. Regularly check in with your emotions around money
5. Celebrate financial wins, no matter how small

Remember, seeking help from a financial therapist or counselor is a sign of strength, not weakness. It's like going to the gym for your financial mental health!

The Link Between Physical Health and Financial Wellness

It's not just your mental health that's affected by your financial situation. Your physical health can also take a hit when you're under financial stress. Here's how:

1. Chronic Stress: Financial worries can lead to chronic stress, which has been linked to a host of health issues including heart disease, high blood pressure, and a weakened immune system.
2. Sleep Disturbances: Money worries can keep you up at night, leading to sleep deprivation. This can affect your cognitive function, mood, and overall health.
3. Unhealthy Coping Mechanisms: Financial stress might lead to unhealthy coping mechanisms like overeating, excessive drinking, or smoking, all of which can negatively impact your health.
4. Delayed Medical Care: When money is tight, people often put off necessary medical care, which can lead to more serious health issues down the line.
5. Poor Nutrition: Financial constraints might lead to choosing cheaper, less nutritious food options, which can affect your overall health and well-being.

The good news is that improving your financial wellness can have positive effects on your physical health. As you reduce financial stress, you may find improvements in your sleep, energy levels, and overall well-being.

Cultural Considerations in Financial Wellness

It's important to recognize that financial wellness can look different across various cultural contexts. Here are some considerations:

1. Collective vs. Individual Financial Responsibility: In some cultures, financial responsibilities are shared among extended family members. This can impact how individuals approach personal finance and financial stress.
2. Money Taboos: Some cultures consider discussing money to be taboo, which can hinder open communication about finances. Recognizing and respectfully navigating these cultural norms is crucial.
3. Cultural Values and Financial Goals: Different cultures may prioritize different financial goals. For example, some may place higher importance on homeownership, while others might prioritize entrepreneurship or supporting extended family.
4. Generational Differences: Within cultures, there can be significant differences in financial attitudes between generations, particularly in immigrant families.

5. Religious Considerations: Some religions have specific guidelines around money and finance, which can influence financial decisions and attitudes.

When addressing financial wellness, it's important to be sensitive to these cultural factors and adapt strategies accordingly.

The Future of Financial Wellness: Trends to Watch

As we look to the future, several exciting trends are emerging in the field of financial wellness:

1. AI-Powered Financial Coaching: Imagine having a 24/7 financial coach powered by artificial intelligence. These AI coaches will provide personalized advice, emotional support, and even detect signs of financial stress based on your spending patterns.
2. Virtual Reality Financial Therapy: VR technology may soon allow us to confront our money fears in immersive, controlled environments. Picture facing your fear of investing in a virtual stock market where the stakes are low but the learning is high.

3. Biometric Stress Monitoring: Wearable devices may soon be able to detect financial stress through physical indicators like heart rate and skin conductivity, prompting interventions before stress escalates.
4. Gamification of Financial Wellness: Expect to see more apps and programs that turn financial wellness into a fun, rewarding game. Leveling up your savings might earn you real-world rewards!
5. Workplace Financial Wellness Programs: More companies are recognizing the link between financial stress and productivity. Look for comprehensive financial wellness programs becoming a standard employee benefit.
6. Personalized Financial Education: AI and machine learning will enable highly personalized financial education programs tailored to individual learning styles, financial situations, and goals.
7. Integration of Financial and Mental Health Services: We may see more holistic approaches that combine financial planning with mental health support, recognizing the intricate connection between the two.

Quick Start Guide: Your Financial Wellness Action Plan

Ready to boost your financial wellness? Here's a quick start guide to get you on the path to financial peace of mind:

1. Start a daily gratitude practice focused on your finances
2. Download a mindfulness app and use it before making financial decisions
3. Create a "money date" with yourself or your partner to regularly review your finances
4. Identify one negative money belief you have and challenge it
5. Set up automatic savings to reduce financial decision fatigue
6. Reach out to a trusted friend or professional to discuss any financial concerns
7. Practice self-care when dealing with financial stress (deep breathing, exercise, etc.)
8. Commit to learning one new financial concept each week
9. Review and update your budget to ensure it aligns with your values and goals
10. Celebrate a small financial win, no matter how minor it may seem

Self-Assessment Quiz: Your Financial Wellness Check-Up

Rate each statement on a scale of 1 (Strongly Disagree) to 5 (Strongly Agree):

1. I feel in control of my financial situation.
2. I have a clear understanding of my current financial state.
3. I have specific, written financial goals.
4. I regularly track my income and expenses.
5. I have an emergency fund that could cover 3-6 months of expenses.
6. I feel comfortable discussing money with my partner/family.
7. I have a plan to reach my long-term financial goals.
8. I feel confident in my ability to make financial decisions.
9. I rarely lose sleep over financial concerns.
10. I have a positive relationship with money.

Scoring:

1. 40-50: Financial Wellness Warrior - You're on top of your game! Your financial health is in great shape, but remember to stay vigilant and continue learning.

2. 30-39: On the Right Track - You're doing well, but there's room for improvement. Focus on the areas where you scored lower.
3. 20-29: Financial Wellness Work in Progress - Time to focus on your financial health. Consider seeking additional resources or professional advice.
4. Below 20: Financial Wellness Wake-Up Call - It's time to prioritize your financial well-being. Don't be discouraged; everyone starts somewhere!

Remember, this quiz is just a starting point. Use your results to identify areas where you can improve your financial wellness and mental health.

The Physical Impact of Financial Stress

While we've discussed the mental and emotional toll of financial stress, it's crucial to understand that it can also manifest physically. Here's how financial stress can affect your body:

1. Sleep Disturbances: Worrying about money can lead to insomnia or poor sleep quality, which can have cascading effects on your overall health.

2. Cardiovascular Issues: Chronic stress, including financial stress, can contribute to high blood pressure and increase the risk of heart disease.
3. Digestive Problems: Stress can exacerbate conditions like irritable bowel syndrome (IBS) or lead to stomach ulcers.
4. Weakened Immune System: Prolonged stress can suppress your immune function, making you more susceptible to illnesses.
5. Muscle Tension and Pain: Financial stress often leads to physical tension, particularly in the neck, shoulders, and back.
6. Headaches: Stress-induced tension headaches or migraines are common among those experiencing financial worries.
7. Weight Changes: Some people may overeat due to stress, while others might lose their appetite, leading to unhealthy weight fluctuations.

Recognizing these physical symptoms is the first step in addressing both your financial and overall health. If you're experiencing any of these symptoms persistently, it's important to consult with a healthcare professional.

Mindfulness and Financial Wellness

Incorporating mindfulness practices into your financial life can significantly reduce stress and improve your overall well-being. Here are some techniques to try:

1. Mindful Spending: Before making a purchase, take a moment to breathe and ask yourself if this aligns with your values and goals.
2. Gratitude Practice: Regularly acknowledge what you're financially grateful for, no matter how small.
3. Financial Meditation: Set aside time to visualize your financial goals and cultivate a sense of abundance.
4. Mindful Budgeting: Approach budgeting as a form of self-care rather than a restrictive practice.
5. Body Scan: Use this technique to release tension related to financial stress.
6. Mindful Decision-Making: When faced with financial decisions, take time to pause and consider all options without judgment.

Incorporating these practices can help you develop a healthier relationship with money and reduce the emotional impact of financial stress.

Building a Financial Support System

Having a strong support system is crucial for maintaining financial wellness and mental health. Here's how to build and utilize your financial support network:

1. Find a Money Buddy: Partner with a friend who shares similar financial goals. You can hold each other accountable and celebrate wins together.
2. Join a Financial Support Group: Look for local or online groups focused on financial wellness and mental health.
3. Seek Professional Help: Don't hesitate to work with a financial advisor or therapist specializing in financial stress.
4. Engage Your Family: Have open discussions about finances with your partner or family members to ensure you're all on the same page.
5. Utilize Workplace Resources: Many employers offer financial wellness programs or Employee Assistance Programs (EAPs) that can provide support.
6. Connect with Online Communities: Join forums or social media groups focused on financial wellness, but be cautious about following advice without verification.

Remember, seeking support is a sign of strength, not weakness. Building a robust support system can provide you with encouragement, advice, and accountability on your financial wellness journey.

The Future of Financial Wellness Technology

As we look to the future, technology continues to play an increasingly significant role in financial wellness. Here are some emerging trends to watch:

1. AI-Powered Financial Coaching: Artificial Intelligence is being used to provide personalized financial advice and emotional support.
2. Virtual Reality Financial Education: VR technology may soon offer immersive experiences to teach complex financial concepts.
3. Biometric Stress Monitoring: Wearable devices may soon be able to detect financial stress through physical indicators and provide real-time coping strategies.
4. Gamification of Financial Wellness: Expect to see more apps and programs that turn financial wellness into an engaging, rewarding game.

5. Integrated Financial and Mental Health Platforms: Future apps may combine financial management tools with mental health resources for a holistic approach to wellness.
6. Blockchain for Financial Transparency: Blockchain technology could revolutionize how we track and manage our finances, providing unprecedented transparency and security.

While these technologies offer exciting possibilities, it's important to remember that they are tools to support, not replace, your personal financial journey. The key is to find the right balance of technology and personal effort that works for you.

Conclusion: Your Journey to Financial Zen

Congratulations on taking this important step towards improving your financial wellness and mental health! Remember, this journey is a marathon, not a sprint. Be patient with yourself, celebrate your progress, and don't forget to breathe.

As you continue on your path to financial mastery, keep in mind that true wealth isn't just about the numbers in your bank account. It's about creating a life of purpose, joy, and yes, financial peace of mind. You've got this!

In our next and final chapter, we'll explore how to future-proof your finances in an ever-changing world. Get ready to become a financial time traveler

Chapter 10: Future-Proofing Your Finances

Welcome to the final chapter of our journey towards financial mastery in the modern age! We've covered a lot of ground, from rewiring your money mindset to navigating the complexities of investing in the digital era. Now, it's time to look ahead and prepare for the financial landscape of tomorrow. In this chapter, we'll explore how to future-proof your finances, ensuring that you're ready for whatever economic changes and emerging trends come your way.

Understanding the Changing Nature of Work and Income

The world of work is evolving at a breakneck pace, driven by technological advancements, shifting societal values, and global events like the recent pandemic. To secure your financial future, it's crucial to understand these changes and adapt accordingly.

The Rise of Remote Work and Its Financial Implications

Remote work, once considered a perk, has become a mainstream reality for many. According to a 2024 study by Global Workplace Analytics, 25-30% of the workforce is now working from home multiple days a week. This shift has significant financial implications:

1. Cost Savings: Remote workers can save an average of $4,000 per year on commuting costs, work attire, and meals out.
2. Geographic Arbitrage: Some remote workers are moving to areas with lower costs of living while maintaining their higher salaries, a trend known as "geographic arbitrage."

3. Home Office Expenses: While there are savings, remote work can also incur new costs, such as setting up a home office or increased utility bills.
4. Tax Implications: Working remotely can affect your tax situation, especially if you work across state lines.

To capitalize on the remote work trend:

1. Negotiate Your Salary: Don't accept a pay cut for working remotely. In fact, use your increased productivity and the company's savings on office space as leverage for a raise.
2. Optimize Your Home Office: Invest in ergonomic furniture and efficient technology to boost your productivity and reduce long-term health costs.
3. Explore Tax Deductions: Consult with a tax professional about potential deductions for your home office expenses.

Preparing for Potential Job Automation

Automation and artificial intelligence are reshaping the job market. A 2024 report by the World Economic Forum predicts that by 2025, 85 million jobs may be displaced by a shift in the division of labor between humans and machines, while 97 million new roles may emerge.

To protect your financial future in the face of automation:

1. Upskill Continuously: Focus on developing skills that are hard to automate, such as creativity, emotional intelligence, and complex problem-solving.
2. Stay Informed: Keep abreast of technological developments in your industry and be prepared to adapt.
3. Consider a Career Pivot: If your current role is at high risk of automation, consider transitioning to a field with more long-term stability.
4. Build an Emergency Fund: Aim for 6-12 months of living expenses to provide a cushion in case of job displacement.

Case Study: The Adaptive Administrative Assistant

Meet Maria, a 35-year-old administrative assistant. When she heard that AI was starting to take over many administrative tasks, she didn't panic – she pivoted. Maria took online courses in data analysis and project management. When her company introduced AI to handle scheduling and basic correspondence, Maria was ready. She transitioned into a role as a project coordinator, using her new skills to analyze project data and manage team workflows. Her proactive approach not only secured her job but also resulted in a 20% salary increase.

Diversifying Income Streams for Greater Stability

In an uncertain job market, relying on a single income source can be risky. Diversifying your income can provide greater financial stability and open up new opportunities.

Case Study: Sarah's Income Diversification Journey

Sarah, a high school English teacher, recognized the need to diversify her income. Here's how she created multiple income streams:

1. Online Tutoring: Sarah began offering online tutoring sessions in the evenings, earning an extra $500 per month.
2. Digital Products: She created and sold downloadable lesson plans and study guides on Teachers Pay Teachers, generating passive income of $300-$400 per month.
3. Online Course: Sarah developed a course on essay writing for college applications, which she sells on Udemy, earning an average of $600 per month.
4. Freelance Writing: She started writing educational content for websites, adding another $400-$500 to her monthly income.

By diversifying her income, Sarah not only increased her earnings but also created a financial safety net and opened up new career possibilities.

Exercise: Brainstorming Additional Income Sources

Take 15 minutes to brainstorm potential additional income sources based on your skills and interests. Consider:

1. What skills do you have that others might pay for?
2. Can you create digital products related to your expertise?
3. Is there a service you could offer on freelance platforms?
4. Could you monetize a hobby or passion?

Remember, the goal is to create income streams that complement your main job and align with your skills and interests.

Exercise: Brainstorming Additional Income Sources

Take 15 minutes to brainstorm potential additional income sources based on your skills and interests. Consider:

1. What skills do you have that others might pay for?
2. Can you create digital products related to your expertise?

3. Is there a service you could offer on freelance platforms?
4. Could you monetize a hobby or passion?

Remember, the goal is to create income streams that complement your main job and align with your skills and interests.

Navigating the Future of Money

The financial world is undergoing a digital revolution, with new technologies and systems emerging at a rapid pace. Understanding these changes is crucial for making informed financial decisions in the years to come.

The Basics of Blockchain and Cryptocurrency

Blockchain technology and cryptocurrencies have moved from the fringes to the mainstream of finance. Here's what you need to know:

Blockchain Basics:

1. Blockchain is a decentralized, digital ledger that records transactions across many computers.
2. It's transparent, secure, and resistant to modification, making it ideal for financial transactions.

Cryptocurrency 101:

1. Cryptocurrencies are digital or virtual currencies that use cryptography for security.
2. Bitcoin, launched in 2009, was the first cryptocurrency, but there are now thousands of others, known as "altcoins."

Key Considerations for Crypto Investing:

1. High Volatility: Cryptocurrency prices can be extremely volatile. Only invest what you can afford to lose.
2. Regulatory Uncertainty: The regulatory landscape for cryptocurrencies is still evolving, which can impact their value and usage.
3. Security Risks: While blockchain itself is secure, cryptocurrency exchanges and wallets can be vulnerable to hacks.
4. Environmental Concerns: Some cryptocurrencies, particularly Bitcoin, have been criticized for their high energy consumption.

If you're considering investing in cryptocurrencies:

1. Start small and educate yourself thoroughly before investing.

2. Use reputable exchanges and secure wallets to store your assets.
3. Consider cryptocurrencies as a small part of a diversified portfolio, not a get-rich-quick scheme.

Case Study: The Cautious Crypto Investor

Meet Alex, a 29-year-old software developer who decided to dip his toes into the crypto waters. Instead of going all-in on Bitcoin, Alex took a more measured approach:

1. Education First: Alex spent three months learning about blockchain technology and different cryptocurrencies before making any investments.
2. Start Small: He began by investing just 2% of his portfolio in a mix of Bitcoin and Ethereum.
3. Dollar-Cost Averaging: Instead of trying to time the market, Alex set up automatic monthly purchases to average out the price over time.
4. Secure Storage: Alex invested in a hardware wallet to securely store his crypto assets offline.
5. Regular Rebalancing: As crypto grew to become a larger portion of his portfolio due to price increases, Alex regularly rebalanced to maintain his desired asset allocation.

The result? While Alex has seen significant volatility in his crypto investments, his cautious approach has allowed him to benefit from the upside while limiting his exposure to potential losses.

The Potential Impact of Central Bank Digital Currencies (CBDCs)

Central Bank Digital Currencies (CBDCs) are digital forms of a country's fiat currency, issued and regulated by the national central bank. As of 2024, several countries are piloting or exploring CBDCs, including China, Sweden, and the Bahamas.

Potential impacts of CBDCs:

1. Faster, Cheaper Transactions: CBDCs could make domestic and cross-border payments quicker and less expensive.
2. Financial Inclusion: They could provide banking services to the unbanked population.
3. Monetary Policy: CBDCs could give central banks new tools for implementing monetary policy.
4. Privacy Concerns: The traceability of digital currencies raises questions about financial privacy.

As CBDCs develop, consider:

1. How they might affect your banking and investment strategies.
2. The potential impact on traditional banking services.
3. Privacy implications and how to protect your financial data.

The Rise of Decentralized Finance (DeFi) and Its Opportunities

Decentralized Finance, or DeFi, refers to financial services built on blockchain technology that operate without traditional intermediaries like banks or brokerages.

Key DeFi concepts:

1. Smart Contracts: Self-executing contracts with the terms directly written into code.
2. Decentralized Exchanges (DEXs): Platforms for trading cryptocurrencies without a central authority.
3. Yield Farming: Lending or staking cryptocurrency to earn returns.
4. Liquidity Mining: Providing liquidity to DeFi protocols in exchange for rewards.

Potential opportunities in DeFi:

1. Higher yields on savings compared to traditional banks.
2. Access to financial services without needing a bank account.
3. New investment opportunities in emerging DeFi projects.

However, DeFi also comes with significant risks, including:

1. Smart contract vulnerabilities.
2. High volatility and potential for significant losses.
3. Regulatory uncertainty.

If you're interested in exploring DeFi:

1. Start with small amounts to understand the systems.
2. Thoroughly research any platform or project before investing.
3. Be prepared for high volatility and potential losses.

Exercise: Researching Emerging Fintech Trends

Choose one emerging fintech trend (e.g., CBDCs, DeFi, or a specific cryptocurrency) and spend 30 minutes researching its potential impact on personal finance. Consider:

1. How might this technology change the way you manage money?
2. What are the potential benefits and risks?
3. How could you incorporate this trend into your financial strategy?

Write a brief summary of your findings and how you might adapt your financial plans in response to this trend.

Climate Change and Your Finances: Preparing for a Warming World

Climate change isn't just an environmental issue – it's a financial one too. As the world heats up, so does the need to climate-proof your finances. Let's explore how climate change might impact your wallet and what you can do about it.

The Financial Impacts of Climate Change

1. Insurance Costs: As extreme weather events become more frequent, insurance premiums for homes and vehicles are likely to rise. In some high-risk areas, insurance might become unavailable or prohibitively expensive.
2. Property Values: Areas prone to flooding, wildfires, or other climate-related risks may see decreasing

property values. On the flip side, areas less affected by climate change might see property values increase.
3. Energy Costs: Extreme temperatures could lead to higher heating and cooling costs. However, the transition to renewable energy might lead to long-term savings.
4. Food Prices: Changing weather patterns and extreme events can affect crop yields, potentially increasing food prices.
5. Health Costs: Climate change can exacerbate certain health conditions, potentially leading to increased healthcare costs.
6. Job Market Shifts: Some industries may decline due to climate change, while others (like renewable energy) may see growth.
7. Investment Risks: Certain industries may face increased regulatory pressures or physical risks from climate change.
8. Infrastructure Costs: Communities may need to invest in climate-resilient infrastructure, potentially impacting local taxes and property values.

Case Study: The Climate-Conscious Homeowner

Meet the Johnsons, a family of four living in coastal Florida. After their home was damaged by a hurricane in 2023, they decided to take a proactive approach to climate-proofing their finances:

1. Home Upgrades: They invested in hurricane-resistant windows and a reinforced roof, which not only increased their home's resilience but also lowered their insurance premiums.
2. Insurance Review: They worked with an insurance broker to ensure they had adequate coverage for flood and wind damage.
3. Energy Efficiency: The Johnsons installed solar panels and improved their home's insulation, reducing their energy bills by 40%.
4. Diversified Investments: They shifted some of their investments into climate-resilient sectors and green bonds.
5. Emergency Fund: They built up a larger emergency fund to cover potential climate-related expenses.
6. Career Planning: Mr. Johnson, who worked in the tourism industry, began taking courses in sustainable tourism to future-proof his career.

The result? While they can't control the weather, the Johnsons feel more financially prepared for whatever climate challenges come their way.

Strategies for Climate-Proofing Your Finances

1. Review Your Insurance: Ensure you have adequate coverage for climate-related risks in your area. Consider additional policies like flood insurance if needed.
2. Invest in Resilience: Make your home more resilient to extreme weather events. This can protect your property value and potentially lower insurance costs.
3. Diversify Investments: Consider adding climate-resilient sectors to your investment portfolio. Look into ESG (Environmental, Social, and Governance) funds or green bonds.
4. Plan for Higher Costs: Build some cushion into your budget for potentially higher food, energy, and insurance costs.
5. Location, Location, Location: When buying property, consider long-term climate projections for the area.
6. Career Planning: Stay informed about how climate change might affect your industry. Consider developing skills in growing, climate-resilient sectors.
7. Support Climate Action: Advocate for climate policies that can mitigate long-term financial risks.

Exercise: Climate Risk Assessment

Take 15 minutes to assess your personal climate-related financial risks:

1. Research climate projections for your area. What risks (e.g., flooding, heat waves, wildfires) are most likely?
2. Review your insurance policies. Do they adequately cover climate-related risks?
3. Look at your investment portfolio. How exposed are you to climate-vulnerable sectors?
4. Brainstorm three actions you could take in the next year to reduce your climate-related financial risks.

Remember, while climate change presents significant challenges, being proactive can help protect your financial future.

Planning for Long-Term Care and Healthcare Costs

As life expectancies increase, planning for healthcare and long-term care costs in retirement becomes increasingly important. Let's explore strategies to prepare for these potential major expenses.

Understanding Long-Term Care Insurance Options

Long-term care (LTC) insurance helps cover the costs of care when you have a chronic medical condition, disability, or disorder. Given that 70% of people turning 65 can expect to use some form of long-term care during their lives, according to the U.S. Department of Health and Human Services, it's crucial to understand your options.

Types of Long-Term Care Insurance:

1. Traditional LTC Insurance:
2. Pros: Comprehensive coverage, potentially lower premiums if purchased early.
3. Cons: Use-it-or-lose-it policy, premiums may increase over time.
4. Hybrid Life Insurance/LTC Policies:
5. Pros: Provides both life insurance and LTC coverage, guarantees some payout.
6. Cons: Higher upfront costs, may offer less comprehensive LTC coverage.
7. Short-Term Care Insurance:
8. Pros: Lower premiums, easier to qualify for.
9. Cons: Limited coverage period (typically up to one year).

When considering LTC insurance:

1. Start researching in your 50s or early 60s.
2. Compare policies from multiple providers.
3. Consider your family health history and potential care needs.
4. Evaluate the financial strength of the insurance company.

Strategies for Saving for Healthcare Costs in Retirement

Healthcare costs can be one of the largest expenses in retirement. Fidelity estimates that an average retired couple age 65 in 2024 may need approximately $315,000 saved (after tax) to cover health care expenses in retirement.

Strategies to save for healthcare costs:

1. Maximize Health Savings Account (HSA) Contributions:
2. HSAs offer triple tax advantages: tax-deductible contributions, tax-free growth, and tax-free withdrawals for qualified medical expenses.
3. In 2024, individuals can contribute up to $3,850 and families up to $7,750, with an additional $1,000 catch-up contribution for those 55 and older.
4. Consider a Medicare Supplement (Medigap) Policy:

5. These policies can help cover out-of-pocket costs not covered by Original Medicare.
6. Budget for Medicare Premiums:
7. Remember that while Medicare provides coverage, it's not free. Budget for premiums, deductibles, and copayments.
8. Invest in Preventive Care:
9. Regular check-ups and a healthy lifestyle can help reduce future healthcare costs.
10. Create a Dedicated Healthcare Savings Fund:
11. Consider setting aside a portion of your retirement savings specifically for healthcare expenses.

Case Study: The Health-Savvy Retiree

Meet Robert, a 68-year-old retiree who took proactive steps to manage his healthcare costs:

1. HSA Maximization: Robert maximized his HSA contributions for years before retiring, building a significant tax-free fund for healthcare expenses.
2. Long-Term Care Planning: He and his wife purchased a joint long-term care insurance policy in their 50s.
3. Medicare Planning: Robert researched and chose a Medicare Advantage plan that best fit his health needs and budget.

4. Healthy Lifestyle: He committed to regular exercise and a healthy diet, potentially reducing future healthcare needs.
5. Healthcare Budget: Robert includes anticipated healthcare costs in his annual retirement budget, adjusting for inflation each year.

The result? While healthcare costs are still significant, Robert feels prepared and less anxious about managing these expenses in retirement.

The Role of Health Savings Accounts (HSAs) in Long-Term Planning

Health Savings Accounts (HSAs) can be a powerful tool for long-term financial planning, especially for healthcare costs in retirement.

Key features of HSAs:

1. Contributions are tax-deductible.
2. Growth is tax-free.
3. Withdrawals for qualified medical expenses are tax-free.
4. Unlike Flexible Spending Accounts (FSAs), HSA funds roll over year to year.

5. After age 65, you can withdraw funds for non-medical expenses without penalty (though you'll pay income tax on these withdrawals).

Strategies for maximizing your HSA:

1. Contribute the Maximum: If possible, contribute the annual maximum to your HSA.
2. Invest Your HSA Funds: Many HSAs allow you to invest your funds in mutual funds or other investments, potentially growing your balance over time.
3. Pay Current Medical Expenses Out-of-Pocket: If you can afford to, pay current medical expenses out-of-pocket and let your HSA balance grow for future use.
4. Keep Records of Medical Expenses: Even if you pay out-of-pocket now, you can reimburse yourself from your HSA in the future, as long as you have records of the expenses.

Exercise: Calculating Potential Long-Term Care Costs

Use an online long-term care cost calculator (many insurance companies provide these on their websites) to estimate potential long-term care costs based on your family history and location. Consider:

1. The average cost of care in your area.
2. How long you might need care (consider family history of longevity and health conditions).
3. How much of these potential costs you could cover from your current retirement savings.
4. Whether long-term care insurance might be appropriate for your situation.

The Gig Economy and Freelance Work: Financial Strategies for the New Work Paradigm

The gig economy continues to grow, with more people choosing freelance or contract work over traditional employment. While this offers flexibility and opportunities, it also presents unique financial challenges.

Key financial strategies for gig workers and freelancers:

1. Create a Stable Budget:
2. Plan for income fluctuations by basing your budget on your lowest earning months.
3. Set aside a portion of higher-earning months to cover leaner periods.
4. Save for Taxes:
5. Set aside 25-30% of your income for taxes, as you'll be responsible for both the employee and employer portions of Social Security and Medicare taxes.
6. Make quarterly estimated tax payments to avoid penalties.
7. Build a Robust Emergency Fund:
8. Aim for 6-12 months of living expenses, given the potential for income volatility.
9. Invest in Retirement:

10. Consider a Solo 401(k) or SEP IRA, which often allow for higher contribution limits than traditional IRAs.
11. Obtain Proper Insurance:
12. Look into health insurance options, including ACA marketplace plans or professional association group plans.
13. Consider disability insurance to protect your income.
14. Separate Business and Personal Finances:
15. Open a separate business checking account and credit card to simplify accounting and tax preparation.
16. Invest in Your Skills:
17. Continually update your skills to remain competitive in the gig economy.

Case Study: The Successful Freelancer

Meet Alex, a 32-year-old graphic designer who transitioned from a full-time job to freelancing:

1. Diverse Income Streams: Alex developed multiple income streams, including client work, online course creation, and selling digital assets.
2. Financial Buffer: He built a 6-month emergency fund before going full-time freelance.

3. Tax Strategy: Alex works with an accountant to manage quarterly tax payments and maximize deductions.
4. Retirement Planning: He opened a Solo 401(k) and consistently contributes a percentage of his income.
5. Health Insurance: Alex found an affordable health insurance plan through his local freelancers' association.
6. Continuous Learning: He allocates a portion of his budget for courses and conferences to stay current in his field.

The result? Two years into full-time freelancing, Alex has a more stable income than he did in his corporate job, with the added benefits of flexibility and job satisfaction.

Artificial Intelligence and Personal Finance

Artificial Intelligence (AI) is increasingly influencing the world of personal finance. Understanding how to leverage AI tools while being aware of their limitations can help you make more informed financial decisions.

Ways AI is impacting personal finance:

1. Robo-Advisors:
2. AI-driven investment platforms that create and manage portfolios based on your risk tolerance and goals.
3. Pros: Lower fees, accessible with small amounts of capital.
4. Cons: May not be suitable for complex financial situations.
5. Budgeting and Spending Analysis:
6. AI-powered apps can categorize your spending, identify patterns, and suggest areas for savings.
7. Fraud Detection:
8. Banks and credit card companies use AI to detect unusual patterns that might indicate fraud.
9. Credit Decisions:
10. Some lenders use AI to assess creditworthiness, potentially opening up credit access to those with limited credit histories.
11. Personalized Financial Advice:
12. AI chatbots and virtual assistants can provide basic financial advice and answer questions.

While AI offers many benefits, it's important to:

1. Understand the limitations of AI-driven advice.
2. Keep your personal financial data secure when using AI-powered tools.

3. Use AI as a supplement to, not a replacement for, human financial advice when dealing with complex situations.

The Rise of Sustainable Finance

As awareness of environmental and social issues grows, sustainable finance is becoming increasingly important. This trend encompasses various approaches to investing and financial decision-making that consider environmental, social, and governance (ESG) factors.

Key Aspects of Sustainable Finance:

1. ESG Investing: Incorporating environmental, social, and governance factors into investment decisions.
2. Green Bonds: Fixed-income securities that fund projects with environmental benefits.
3. Impact Investing: Investing with the intention to generate positive, measurable social and environmental impact alongside financial returns.

4. Sustainable Banking: Financial institutions offering products and services that support sustainable development.

According to a 2024 report by Bloomberg Intelligence, global ESG assets are on track to exceed $50 trillion by 2025, representing more than a third of the projected total assets under management.

How to Incorporate Sustainable Finance into Your Strategy:

1. Research ESG Funds: Look for mutual funds or ETFs that align with your values and financial goals.
2. Consider Green Bonds: These can provide fixed income while supporting environmental projects.
3. Explore Sustainable Banking Options: Some banks offer accounts and services focused on sustainability.
4. Engage with Companies: Use your shareholder voice to advocate for sustainable practices.

Remember, sustainable investing doesn't mean sacrificing returns. Many studies have shown that ESG-focused investments can perform as well as or better than traditional investments over the long term.

Preparing for Potential Economic Shifts

The global economy is constantly evolving, and being prepared for potential shifts is crucial for long-term financial stability. Here are some strategies to consider:

1. Diversification: This remains one of the most effective strategies for managing risk. Spread your investments across different asset classes, sectors, and geographic regions.
2. Build a Robust Emergency Fund: Aim for 6-12 months of living expenses in easily accessible savings. This can provide a buffer during economic downturns or personal financial setbacks.
3. Continuous Skill Development: In a rapidly changing job market, continuous learning and skill development can increase your employability and income potential.
4. Consider Alternative Income Streams: Developing multiple income sources can provide financial stability if one stream is disrupted.
5. Stay Informed: Keep up with economic trends and policy changes that could impact your finances.
6. Debt Management: Prioritize paying off high-interest debt and be cautious about taking on new debt.

7. Flexible Financial Planning: Be prepared to adjust your financial plans as economic conditions change.

The Future of Retirement Planning

Traditional concepts of retirement are evolving, influenced by longer life expectancies, changing work patterns, and economic uncertainties. Here's how to adapt your retirement planning for the future:

1. Longevity Planning: With increasing life expectancies, plan for a potentially longer retirement period.
2. Phased Retirement: Consider a gradual transition from full-time work to retirement, which can provide both financial and psychological benefits.
3. Health Care Costs: Factor in potentially higher health care costs in retirement, including long-term care expenses.
4. Social Security Considerations: Stay informed about potential changes to Social Security and factor these into your planning.
5. Technology and Retirement: Leverage digital tools for retirement planning and management.
6. Continued Income Streams: Explore options for generating income in retirement, such as part-time work, consulting, or rental income.

7. Global Retirement Options: Consider the potential for retiring abroad where costs may be lower.

Case Study: The New Retirement

Meet Maria, a 55-year-old marketing executive. Instead of a traditional retirement at 65, Maria is planning a phased approach:

1. At 60, she'll reduce her full-time work to 3 days a week, using the extra time to start a small online business.
2. At 65, she'll fully retire from her marketing career but continue running her online business.
3. She's also considering spending part of the year in a country with a lower cost of living to stretch her retirement savings.

Maria's approach illustrates how retirement is becoming more flexible and personalized, combining traditional retirement savings with continued income streams and lifestyle adjustments.

Embracing Financial Technology

As we look to the future, financial technology (fintech) will play an increasingly important role in personal finance management. Here's how to leverage fintech to future-proof your finances:

1. Digital Banking: Embrace online and mobile banking for convenience and better tracking of your finances.
2. Budgeting Apps: Use apps like Mint or YNAB to track spending and stick to a budget.
3. Robo-Advisors: Consider using robo-advisors for low-cost, automated investment management.
4. Peer-to-Peer Lending: Explore P2P lending platforms for potentially higher returns on your investments or as an alternative borrowing option.
5. Digital Wallets: Familiarize yourself with digital payment methods for convenience and security.
6. Cryptocurrency: While volatile, understanding and potentially investing a small portion in cryptocurrency could be part of a diversified portfolio.
7. Personal Finance Management Platforms: Use comprehensive platforms that integrate all your financial accounts for a holistic view of your finances.

Remember, while fintech can provide powerful tools, it's important to understand the technology you're using and ensure you're comfortable with the level of data sharing involved.

Quick Start Guide: Future-Proofing Your Finances

Ready to start future-proofing your finances? Here's a quick start guide:

1. Assess Your Current Financial Situation: Take stock of your assets, debts, income, and expenses.
2. Set Long-Term Financial Goals: Define what financial security looks like for you in 10, 20, or 30 years.
3. Create a Flexible Budget: Develop a budget that allows for saving and investing while maintaining flexibility for life changes.

4. Start or Increase Your Emergency Fund: Aim for 3-6 months of living expenses in easily accessible savings.
5. Review Your Investment Strategy: Ensure your investment portfolio is diversified and aligned with your long-term goals and risk tolerance.
6. Explore Sustainable Investing Options: Look into ESG funds or other sustainable investing options that align with your values.
7. Educate Yourself on Emerging Financial Technologies: Stay informed about fintech developments that could benefit your financial management.
8. Consider Long-Term Care Insurance: Research options and determine if it's appropriate for your situation.
9. Develop Multiple Income Streams: Look for ways to diversify your income through side hustles, passive income, or investments.
10. Continuously Educate Yourself: Stay informed about economic trends, policy changes, and new financial products that could impact your financial future.

Self-Assessment Quiz: How Future-Proof Are Your Finances?

Rate each statement on a scale of 1 (Strongly Disagree) to 5 (Strongly Agree):

1. I have a clear understanding of my long-term financial goals.
2. My investment portfolio is well-diversified across different asset classes and sectors.
3. I regularly review and update my financial plans based on economic changes and personal circumstances.
4. I have a solid emergency fund that could cover 3-6 months of expenses.

5. I'm actively developing my skills to stay relevant in the changing job market.
6. I've considered the potential impact of climate change on my finances and investments.
7. I'm familiar with and use various fintech tools to manage my finances.
8. I've explored sustainable or ESG investing options.
9. I have a plan for potential long-term care needs in the future.
10. I'm actively working on developing multiple income streams.

Scoring:

1. 40-50: Financial Future Master - You're well-prepared for future financial challenges!
2. 30-39: On the Right Track - You're doing well, but there's room for improvement in some areas.
3. 20-29: Future-Proofing Beginner - It's time to focus more on preparing your finances for the future.
4. Below 20: Financial Future Wake-Up Call - Start implementing future-proofing strategies today!

Conclusion: Embracing the Future of Finance

As we've explored in this chapter, the financial landscape is constantly evolving, shaped by technological advancements, economic shifts, and changing societal values. By staying informed, adaptable, and proactive in your financial planning, you can navigate these changes and build a secure financial future.

Remember, future-proofing your finances isn't about predicting the future with certainty – it's about building resilience and flexibility into your financial plan. This allows you to adapt to whatever changes come your way, whether it's a shift in the job market, new investment opportunities, or unexpected global events.

As you move forward, continue to educate yourself about emerging trends in finance, regularly review and adjust your financial plans, and don't hesitate to seek professional advice when needed. With the right strategies and mindset, you can face the future with financial confidence and security. In our next and final chapter, we'll bring together all the concepts we've covered throughout the book and provide a comprehensive roadmap for achieving financial mastery in the modern age. Get ready to put all your new knowledge into action!

Conclusion: Your Roadmap to Financial Mastery

Congratulations, financial ninja! You've made it to the end of our wild ride through the world of personal finance. If you've stuck with me this far, you're well on your way to becoming a true master of your money. But before you go off to conquer the financial world, let's take a moment to recap our journey and chart your course forward.

The Journey So Far: Key Lessons from Each Chapter

Chapter 1: Rewiring Your Money Mindset

Remember when we talked about your brain being your most powerful financial tool? Well, it's true! We learned that your money mindset - those deeply ingrained beliefs and attitudes about money - can make or break your financial success. We explored how to identify and challenge those sneaky limiting beliefs that have been holding you back.

Key takeaways:

1. Your money mindset is shaped by your past experiences, but it's not set in stone.
2. Cultivating a growth mindset around money opens up new possibilities for financial success.
3. Practicing gratitude and positive affirmations can help rewire your brain for abundance.

Remember Sarah, who transformed her scarcity mindset into one of abundance? By shifting her perspective, she not only improved her finances but also her overall quality of life. You too can make this powerful shift!

Chapter 2: Mastering the Art of Mindful Spending

We dove deep into the world of mindful spending, where every dollar you spend aligns with your values and goals. It's not about depriving yourself, but about making intentional choices that bring you joy and move you closer to your financial dreams.

Key takeaways:

1. Create a values-based spending plan that reflects what truly matters to you.
2. Use technology to your advantage with budgeting apps and expense trackers.
3. Implement the 50/30/20 rule: 50% for needs, 30% for wants, and 20% for savings and debt repayment.

Remember Alex, who used mindful spending techniques to save for his dream vacation while still enjoying his daily latte? That could be you, sipping a piña colada on a beach, knowing you've made it happen through smart, intentional choices.

Chapter 3: Navigating the Debt Maze

We faced the debt monster head-on and came out victorious! We learned that not all debt is created equal and that with the right strategy, you can slay your debt dragon and reclaim your financial freedom.

Key takeaways:

1. Differentiate between good debt (investments in your future) and bad debt (high-interest consumer debt).
2. Choose a debt repayment strategy that works for you: debt avalanche for maximum interest savings or debt snowball for quick wins and motivation.
3. Leverage technology to automate payments and track your progress.

Remember Maria and John, who paid off $50,000 in debt in just two years? Their story shows that with determination and the right tools, financial freedom is within reach.

Chapter 4: Building Your Financial Fortress

We learned that true financial security comes from having a solid foundation - your financial fortress. This isn't just about having an emergency fund (though that's crucial); it's about creating a comprehensive safety net that can weather any storm.

Key takeaways:

1. Build an emergency fund that covers 3-6 months of expenses.
2. Diversify your income streams to create multiple pillars of financial support.
3. Invest in the right insurance to protect yourself and your loved ones.

Think back to Lisa, who used her emergency fund to turn a sudden job loss into an opportunity to start her own business. Your financial fortress isn't just about protection - it's about creating the freedom to seize opportunities when they arise.

Chapter 5: Investing in the Digital Age

We demystified the world of investing and learned how to make our money work for us in the digital age. From robo-advisors to cryptocurrency, we explored how technology is democratizing investing and opening up new opportunities.

Key takeaways:

1. Start investing early and leverage the power of compound interest.

2. Diversify your portfolio to spread risk and maximize potential returns.
3. Stay informed about new investment opportunities, but always do your due diligence.

Remember Chris, who started investing small amounts through a micro-investing app and built a substantial portfolio over time? That could be you, watching your wealth grow with each passing year.

Chapter 6: Mastering the Gig Economy

We embraced the flexibility and opportunities of the gig economy, learning how to thrive in a world of side hustles and freelance work.

Key takeaways:

1. Diversify your income streams to create financial stability.
2. Manage irregular income with a solid budgeting strategy.
3. Take advantage of tax benefits available to gig workers and freelancers.

Think of Emma, who turned her passion for graphic design into a thriving freelance business. The gig economy isn't just about making ends meet - it's about creating a lifestyle that aligns with your values and goals.

Chapter 7: The Art of Career Hacking

We learned how to level up our careers and increase our earning potential through strategic skill development and savvy negotiation.

Key takeaways:

1. Identify and develop high-income skills that are in demand in your industry.
2. Build a personal brand that showcases your unique value proposition.
3. Master the art of salary negotiation to ensure you're paid what you're worth.

Remember Alex, who doubled his income by learning data analytics skills? Your career is your biggest financial asset - invest in it wisely!

Chapter 8: Relationships and Money

We tackled the often tricky topic of money in relationships, learning how to navigate financial decisions with partners and family members.

Key takeaways:

1. Have open and honest conversations about money with your partner.
2. Develop shared financial goals and values.
3. Teach children about money through age-appropriate lessons and activities.

Remember Tom and Sarah, who strengthened their relationship by working together on their finances? Financial harmony can lead to stronger, more fulfilling relationships.

Chapter 9: Financial Wellness and Mental Health

We recognized the crucial link between financial health and mental well-being, learning strategies to reduce financial stress and cultivate a positive money mindset.

Key takeaways:

1. Practice mindfulness and stress-reduction techniques to manage financial anxiety.
2. Seek professional help if financial stress is impacting your mental health.

3. Cultivate a balanced approach to money that prioritizes both financial goals and overall well-being.

Think of James, who overcame his financial anxiety through mindfulness practices and therapy. Your financial journey isn't just about numbers - it's about creating a life of peace and fulfillment.

Chapter 10: Future-Proofing Your Finances

We looked ahead to the future, preparing for economic changes and emerging trends that will shape the financial landscape.

Key takeaways:

1. Stay informed about emerging technologies like blockchain and AI that may impact personal finance.
2. Develop adaptable skills to thrive in a changing job market.
3. Plan for long-term expenses like healthcare and long-term care.

Remember Lisa, who future-proofed her career by learning coding skills? By staying ahead of the curve, you can turn potential challenges into opportunities.

The Importance of Continuous Learning and Adaptation

If there's one overarching lesson from our journey, it's this: the world of personal finance is constantly evolving, and so should you. The strategies that worked for your parents' generation may not be sufficient in today's digital, globalized economy.

Continuous learning isn't just about acquiring new information - it's about developing the ability to adapt to change, to think critically about financial decisions, and to stay resilient in the face of economic uncertainty. It's about cultivating a growth mindset that sees challenges as opportunities for learning and growth.

Here are some ways to make continuous learning a part of your financial life:

1. Stay Informed: Follow reputable financial news sources, subscribe to personal finance podcasts, or join online communities focused on financial education.
2. Experiment and Reflect: Try new financial strategies on a small scale, reflect on the results, and adjust your approach accordingly.

3. Seek Diverse Perspectives: Engage with people from different financial backgrounds and learn from their experiences and strategies.
4. Embrace Technology: Stay open to new financial technologies and tools that can help you manage your money more effectively.
5. Regular Financial Check-ups: Schedule regular reviews of your financial situation and goals, adjusting your strategies as needed.

Remember, financial mastery is not a destination - it's a journey. By committing to continuous learning and adaptation, you're setting yourself up for long-term financial success, no matter what the future holds.

Your Call to Action: Creating a Personalized Financial Mastery Plan

Now that we've recapped our journey through the world of personal finance, it's time for you to take the reins and create your own Personalized Financial Mastery Plan. This plan will be your roadmap to financial success, incorporating the lessons we've learned and tailoring them to your unique situation and goals. Let's break this down into actionable steps:

1. Assess Your Current Financial Situation
2. Calculate your net worth (assets minus liabilities)

3. Track your income and expenses for at least one month
4. Review your credit report and score
5. List all debts, including balances and interest rates
6. Evaluate your current savings and investments
7. Define Your Financial Goals
8. Short-term goals (1-3 years): e.g., building an emergency fund, paying off credit card debt
9. Medium-term goals (3-10 years): e.g., saving for a down payment on a house, starting a business
10. Long-term goals (10+ years): e.g., retirement planning, children's education fund
11. Make each goal SMART (Specific, Measurable, Achievable, Relevant, and Time-bound)
12. Identify Your Financial Priorities Based on your assessment and goals, determine which areas need the most attention:
13. Debt repayment
14. Increasing savings
15. Boosting income
16. Investing for growth
17. Improving financial literacy
18. Create Action Steps for Each Priority For example, if debt repayment is a priority:
19. List debts from highest to lowest interest rate

20. Allocate extra funds to the highest-interest debt while making minimum payments on others
21. Set up automatic payments to avoid late fees
22. Explore balance transfer options for high-interest credit card debt
23. Consider consolidation loans for multiple debts
24. Develop a Realistic Budget
25. Use the 50/30/20 rule as a starting point (50% needs, 30% wants, 20% savings/debt repayment)
26. Identify areas where you can cut expenses
27. Allocate funds to your priority areas
28. Set up a system to track your spending (e.g., budgeting app, spreadsheet)
29. Create an Investment Strategy
30. Determine your risk tolerance
31. Set your asset allocation based on your goals and risk tolerance
32. Choose investment vehicles (e.g., index funds, ETFs, individual stocks)
33. Set up automatic investments to take advantage of dollar-cost averaging
34. Implement Protection Strategies
35. Review and update insurance policies (health, life, disability, property)
36. Create or update your will and estate plan
37. Set up a power of attorney and healthcare directive

38. Plan for Continuous Learning
39. Subscribe to financial newsletters or podcasts
40. Commit to reading one personal finance book per quarter
41. Attend financial workshops or webinars
42. Consider working with a financial advisor for personalized guidance
43. Set Milestones and Rewards
44. Break larger goals into smaller, achievable milestones
45. Set specific dates for achieving these milestones
46. Plan rewards for when you reach each milestone (ensure the rewards don't derail your financial progress)
47. Schedule Regular Reviews
48. Monthly: Review budget and spending
49. Quarterly: Assess progress towards goals, rebalance investments if needed
50. Annually: Comprehensive review of entire financial plan, update goals as needed
51. Develop Multiple Income Streams
52. Explore side hustle opportunities in your field of expertise
53. Consider passive income sources (e.g., rental property, dividend-paying stocks)

54. Invest in developing high-income skills to increase your earning potential
55. Create a Financial Emergency Plan
56. Build an emergency fund covering 3-6 months of expenses
57. Develop a plan for potential job loss or income reduction
58. Create a list of non-essential expenses that can be cut quickly if needed

Remember, your Financial Mastery Plan is a living document. It should evolve as you grow and as your circumstances change. The key is to stay committed to your financial growth and to keep taking action towards your goals. Review and adjust your plan regularly, celebrating your successes along the way.

By following this detailed roadmap, you're not just creating a plan – you're embarking on a journey towards true financial mastery. Stay focused, stay motivated, and remember that every small step brings you closer to your financial goals. You've got this, financial ninja!

Case Study: From Financial Stress to Financial Success

Let's look at how one reader, Jessica, applied the principles from this book to transform her financial life.

Jessica, a 32-year-old marketing manager, was stressed about her finances. She had $30,000 in credit card debt, no savings, and felt like she was living paycheck to paycheck despite a good income. After reading this book, she decided to take control of her finances.

First, Jessica worked on rewiring her money mindset. She realized she had a scarcity mentality and often engaged in emotional spending. By practicing gratitude and positive affirmations daily, she began to shift her perspective.

Next, she created a mindful spending plan. She used a budgeting app to track her expenses and was shocked to see how much she was spending on non-essentials. She implemented the 50/30/20 rule and cut back on unnecessary expenses.

To tackle her debt, Jessica chose the debt avalanche method. She negotiated lower interest rates on her credit cards and set up automatic payments. She also started a side gig as a freelance writer to increase her income and put all extra earnings towards debt repayment.

Jessica built an emergency fund, starting with a goal of $1,000 and gradually increasing it to cover three months of expenses. This gave her peace of mind and prevented her from accumulating more debt when unexpected expenses arose.

She also began investing, starting small with a robo-advisor and gradually learning more about the stock market. She set up automatic investments to take advantage of dollar-cost averaging.

Two years later, Jessica's financial life has been transformed. She's debt-free, has a six-month emergency fund, and is consistently investing for her future. More importantly, she feels confident and in control of her finances.

Jessica's story shows that with the right knowledge, tools, and mindset, anyone can achieve financial success. You too can write your own success story!

Common Pitfalls to Avoid

As you embark on your journey to financial mastery, be aware of these common pitfalls:

1. Trying to Do Too Much at Once: Focus on one or two financial goals at a time to avoid feeling overwhelmed.
2. Neglecting to Track Progress: Regularly review your financial plan and celebrate small wins to stay motivated.
3. Forgetting to Adjust for Life Changes: Major life events like marriage, having children, or changing careers may require adjustments to your financial plan.
4. Ignoring the Emotional Aspect of Money: Remember that financial decisions are often emotional. Be aware of your money emotions and how they influence your choices.
5. Not Seeking Help When Needed: Don't hesitate to consult with financial professionals or seek support from a money buddy when you need guidance.

By being aware of these potential pitfalls, you can navigate around them and stay on track towards your financial goals.

Your Financial Future Starts Now

As we wrap up our journey together, I want to leave you with this thought: your financial future is in your hands. The choices you make today will shape your financial reality tomorrow, next year, and decades from now.

But here's the exciting part - armed with the knowledge and strategies we've explored in this book, you have the power to create the financial future you desire. Whether that's early retirement, starting your own business, buying your dream home, or simply having the peace of mind that comes with financial security, it's all within your reach.

Remember, financial mastery isn't about being perfect. It's about making informed decisions, learning from your experiences, and continuously striving to improve. There will be setbacks along the way - that's part of the journey. But with persistence, adaptability, and the right mindset, you can overcome any financial challenge that comes your way.

Imagine waking up every day feeling confident about your finances. Picture yourself making money decisions with ease, watching your wealth grow, and using your financial success to create a life you love and make a positive impact on the world. That's the power of financial mastery, and it's all possible for you.

So, what are you waiting for? Your journey to financial mastery starts now. Take that first step, whether it's creating your Financial Mastery Plan, opening a savings account, or having a money conversation with your partner. Every action, no matter how small, is a step towards your financial goals.

You've got this, financial ninja. Now go out there and conquer your financial world! Remember, I'm rooting for you every step of the way. Here's to your financial success and the amazing life it will help you create. The future is bright, and it's all yours for the taking!

Your Path to Financial Freedom Starts Here:

If you're ready to take control of your money, embrace AI-powered tools, and create a life of wealth and fulfillment, then Rich in the Making is the book you've been waiting for. The digital revolution is here—will you sit on the sidelines, or will you use it to secure your future?

Your Action Plan for Financial Freedom in the AI-Powered Digital Age:

Rewire Your Money Mindset to overcome self-sabotaging beliefs and adopt a growth-oriented approach to wealth.

Master the Art of Mindful Spending to align your expenses with your values and goals.

Navigate the Debt Maze with proven strategies to eliminate debt and regain control.

Build a Financial Fortress that ensures security for you and your loved ones.

Invest in the Digital Age, including AI tools, fractional shares, robo-advisors, and cryptocurrency opportunities.

Thrive in the Gig Economy, whether you're freelancing, side-hustling, or reinventing your career.

Hustle Smarter with advanced career-hacking techniques to maximize your earning potential.

Balance Financial Wellness and Mental Health for lasting prosperity and happiness.

Future-Proof Your Finances by preparing for AI, blockchain, and the next financial frontier.

Disclaimer

The information provided in this book is for informational purposes only and should not be considered as investment or financial advice. Before making any investment decisions or expenditures, you should seek professional advice from your bank, certified financial advisors, or investment consultancy firms. The content of this book is of a general nature and is not tailored to individual financial circumstances or objectives. Therefore, it should not be relied upon as specific advice for personal investments or expenditures.

Thank you

Jonathan R Whitestone
Eclipse Wolf Publishing

www.ingramcontent.com/pod-product-compliance
Lightning Source LLC
Chambersburg PA
CBHW031604210526
45464CB00004B/1431